An expert entrep
your reac.

ROB STEWART

AUTHORITY

An expert entrepreneur's guide to exploding
your reach, impact and profit

R3THINK PRESS

First published in Great Britain in 2019 by
Rethink Press (www.rethinkpress.com)

What Others Are Saying

Rob's 'sleeves-rolled-up, hands-on' approach has helped us get our first coaching programme off the ground more quickly and more successfully than we ever imagined. We are looking at six figures in year one with more to follow. Can't thank him enough.

     – **Brett Plant**, founder, Oxygen Projects

Rob's book is as powerful as they come. Transparent... practical, cutting edge advice with long-standing, applicable value. Buy this book, you won't regret it.

     – **James Lambert**, James Lambert Coaching

What I love about Rob's book is that it's simple to follow and shares strategies that I can apply to my expert business with ease. It's like the Bible for the expert business owner! Having taken steps to implement Rob's AAA method into my business, I already see the difference that having authority in my niche has. People start watching, then engaging and it's not long before they're knocking at your door!

— **Helen Lane**, co-founder, Vibe Health

Rob has built up an enviable position in the UK expert industry for being known as an authentic, trustable and likable person who has achieved so much in a short space of time. This book teaches you about the processes he went through to get to this stage. When you put into action what Rob tells you to do in this book, it's amazing what becomes possible.

— **Jatinder Spall**, co-founder of JS
Tutoring

This is a clear and illuminating book for anyone who wants to stand out and contribute their knowledge, skills and vision to this fast-changing world of ours. It's practical and simple, with models to follow that will help you understand where you are and how to get to where you want to be. If you have a message, an expertise and a passion to share it, this book will guide you to success without overwhelming you. If you commit to taking the steps laid out in this book, you will build your expert business around your 'authority' with ease and, even better, you may well enjoy it!

— **Helena Holrick**, Chief Cheerleader,
Helping You Shine

Contents

*This book is dedicated to the memory of my beloved
mum, Geri Stewart, whose abundantly generous spirit
taught me the importance of looking after others first.*

Mum, without you, none of this would have been possible.

Foreword

I've known Rob for a number of years now, from a business aspect, as we have been business partners, but also from a social aspect, as we are great friends, so I'm in a great position to give an honest and raw account of the man himself.

As a Royal Air Force (RAF) pilot, you can see his military training in everything he does. He's very structured in his approach to business and that is a major part of his success. After all, all successful businesses are all about structure.

I genuinely don't know anyone else in the expert industry who lives and breathes it as much as Rob. Everything he does is to help his clients become *the* authority in their chosen space. He goes above and beyond to make you a success. It's just his passion.

Rob's advice is invaluable, his passion unwavering and his knowledge unbeatable. He *will* make you the authority in your business.

Listen to Rob and you will succeed. It's as simple as that.

> – **John Paul**, MD, Castledene Sales and Lettings

Introduction

If there's one certainty in any business, it's change. Change in technology, behaviours, the strategies that work, and the roles that become redundant.

Inevitably, change creates opportunity and fear. Some will adapt and thrive; others will wither on the vine. We need only to look at the demise of some of the high-profile and established brands to see this happening right now, all around us.

The change that we are seeing in the expert industry is the symptom of two main causes. Firstly, our markets are craving a different approach: in a world where it's easy to create the perception of a reality that doesn't exist, people are wise to it and desire transparency. Secondly, big changes in media platforms have made it much more difficult to reach people in an organic way – without the need to pay for content distribution. Many experts have been scratching their heads, wondering why they're having to work harder to bring in the same amount of business. On the flip side, a few have noticed the change, adapted and found a solution.

I've experienced this first-hand in the time since I started my first training business, the Property Education Group (PEG), in 2014. Back then, technology was becoming more user-friendly and cheaper for smaller businesses to use, so I decided to build an online presence that focused on systems and automation. This paid dividends: in the second year of trading, my business partner and I achieved sales of almost half a million pounds with just one part-time member of staff and less than £10,000 spent on advertising. But during this time, I spotted some clear trends emerging. As email open rates and organic social media reach dropped dramatically, more competitors entered the market and consumers' expectations shifted. We had to adapt.

In 2016, I set up V Media Global, an agency that helped expert entrepreneurs push through these changes to reach and influence more people in an authentic way. As V Media grew in the new world of the expert entrepreneur, I identified the one thing that caused me to fundamentally change my approach: although we live in a constant state of evolution, some human fundamentals never change. At the core of this is the importance of building a relationship and rapport with your market. And so the Triple A Method was born: a framework for growing your expert business that stands true despite constant change.

This book is written to help you understand and use the Triple A Method in your business, while accelerating the authority and connections you create in your marketplace. It will help you understand the areas outlined below.

The expert industry has changed

The first part of this book explores the biggest revolution the industry has gone through in a decade and looks at why, despite the increase in competition, there has never been more demand for guidance in your market. It also looks at some of the fundamentals of building an expert business today: in particular, the need to focus on building income-producing 'expert assets' that you can leverage, and on designing frameworks rather than worrying about tactics.

Using the Triple A Method

To use the Triple A Method, you need to think long term about your business. While most people focus on lead generation and sales, the key to longevity lies in building awareness and audiences. When you push past the instant gratification trap, you can use the Triple A Method to create:

- **Awareness** of your perfect market's real problems, and how your process solves them

- **Authority** to build your 'intrinsic value' – the perception of what you're really worth – and accelerate the 'know, like, trust' process

- **Automation** to make the most of your expertise, reach more people and create more profits for less work

When all three elements of the Triple A Method come together, you will *amplify* your delivery. Because of that, you need to have a delivery model that you can maximise. This book explains how to make sure of this, focusing on creating a delivery model that delivers maximum profit for the minimum effort.

Building your 'value ecosystem'

The last section of the book explains how to use the Triple A Method in the real world. It shows you how to:

- Craft your power message to cut through the noise and gain attention instantly

- Attract the right audiences quickly and cheaply

- Magnetise them to your message by creating open loops of content

- Prime your audiences to ensure you don't destroy goodwill during the sales process

By the time you have finished reading this book, you will have all the theory, frameworks and practical tools you need to accelerate your reach, visibility and authority in front of your ideal audience. You'll have the foundations in place to build a business that genuinely influences people at scale.

Staying true to yourself

The San Diego to Los Angeles stretch of coastline, where the book was written, is the Mecca of the training industry.

I expected Venice Beach – an iconic place in the Los Angeles region – to be commercialised and developed. In reality, it's one of the most fiercely independent and charismatic stretches of cityscape in the Western world. It attracts an eclectic mix of people, and that's where its joyful feel is derived. From Venice Pier to Santa Monica Pier, the only corporate brand I saw was a lone Baskin Robbins outlet. It looked so aggressively out of place and lonely that I couldn't help but feel sorry for it.

Love or hate this vibe, you cannot deny it. It hits you in the face, takes you out of your comfort zone and makes you wonder where the soul has gone from so much else of what we do.

Key to positioning yourself is to be true to your unique values and be confident enough to show them to the world. This is tough: it stretches you far beyond your comfort zone and creates a blend of fear, excitement and adrenaline. When you put your head above the parapet, you will polarise opinion: some will connect with you deeply and become raving fans, while others will hate everything you stand for and make their view known. But this is how we create our own authority, build intrinsic value and grow as entrepreneurs, leaders and humans.

The beachfront at Venice is lined with old sun-baked musicians, playing their guitars and rocking to the sound of their own voices. In a TV documentary, one of them said that every now and again, fate bestows greatness on a musician and they become a rock star, adored by the world. Everyone else is just a bum with a guitar.

But we now live in a world where you don't need to live in the vain hope that chance will be on your side and you'll 'make it'. You have the right and the ability to reach out and create it yourself by exploding your own authority. Authority is not given; it is earned. The difference between being the most respected, sought-after and highly paid entrepreneur in your space and just being another guy with a smartphone and a Facebook account is merely a state of mind.

This book will help you position yourself as the authority in your space (and sell *a lot* of your products, programmes and services). It teaches you the newest strategies for getting started – with no audience, no list and no existing market presence – and how to rapidly build your intrinsic value so that you become *the* expert in your market. Above all, it will help you achieve something more fundamental: to make a true impact, influence more people in a positive way and bring about change you want to see in the world. When you achieve this, you will also attain a lifestyle that gives you freedom of choice.

Is this really possible? The answer is yes, but there's a step-by-step process that you need to follow to make sure you do it correctly. Without that framework, you could end up shouting at the top of your voice on social media but not actually selling anything. Get it right and you will become the most sought-after authority in your space. You'll never need to worry about where the next client is coming from. You'll be working in flow, creating income streams with a high profit margin while helping others.

You'll have control of your life and how you want to lead it.

CHAPTER ONE

The Expert Industry Has Evolved

O ver the last decade or so, we've seen an explosion in the expert entrepreneur market. Technological progress has removed almost all the barriers to entry: it's never been easier to pick up a laptop, hook it up to a Wi-Fi connection and start your own business by using your experience and expertise to help others. Whether you're a coach, trainer, mentor, speaker or service provider, our industry provides the ultimate in modern business models: low overheads, low barriers, high mobility and flexibility, and the ability to generate high profits while supporting others.

While these changes have made it possible for more of us to join the industry, they have also led to some problems. Firstly, the market has grown so quickly that the space has become busy. Expert entrepreneurs are having to cut through the increasing noise on social media platforms just to get noticed, let alone remembered. At the same time, the continued throttling of organic reach on social media has compounded the problem. Even paying for that reach is becoming more competitive. For example, Facebook has now run out of new advertising space, so more advertisers are competing for a limited resource. The cost of paid ads can only go in one direction, and we are seeing this already. Less organic reach, more competition for ad space and a lot of white noise is making it almost impossible to get your message out to the right people. For many, it seems the only solution is to 'hustle' harder to get noticed, whether in the real or digital world.

The second issue is that our markets have become more sophisticated in their buying behaviours. It's easy to craft a different paradigm of your reality online, and internet marketing has relied heavily on urgency, scarcity and manipulation for a long time. Our markets, however, are starting to reject this, instead craving authenticity and a genuine connection with the people they work with. In this environment, you need to work harder to earn someone's trust; you can't expect people to simply click on your ad, drop in to a webinar and get their credit card out.

The challenge is how to cut through the noise and get noticed in an authentic way that creates genuine connections, while being scalable enough to create a business model that delivers freedom, choice and profit.

Rather than trying to do more, the answer lies in doing less.

Your market needs guidance

There's a reason we've seen an explosion in the expert industry: as the world becomes more complex and fast-paced, there is more need for clarity and direction. The information revolution has given the world virtually unlimited access to data through our smartphones, but this has come with costs.

Our fundamental learning behaviours have changed. Whereas once the challenge was to find information, we now struggle to make sense of an intravenous flow. It's easy to become stuck in overwhelm and procrastination. In the Western world, most of us have the opportunity to learn and do anything we choose to put our mind to – but where do we start?

Let me illustrate with some examples:

- Not long ago, only big businesses, with budgets to match, could put together great-looking websites. Now, anyone can create an account with a software provider and use templates to build their own webpages in minutes. But having the resources to create a website is not the same as understanding how to write effective copy, design good-looking graphics or assemble the page in a flow that converts visitors to clients.

- We now have immediate access to information on hundreds of different diets from around the world: Keto, Paleo, slow carb, Atkins, vegan, fruitarian and so on. But what's the right plan for you? You might read that it's better to eat fewer carbs and more protein, but you might not know how to prepare meals that provide the right nutritional value. Instead, you jump from fad to fad, not getting the results you want, with knock-on effects on other parts of your life.

- In a world dominated by social media and the skewed perception of reality that it creates, it's difficult to focus on achieving one core goal, rather than being distracted by the shiny pennies that are constantly presented to us. When we're exposed to other people's pseudo-realities, it is natural to question our own abilities if we're not experiencing the same results, or pivot as we see someone doing well in another industry. Neither leads to much success.

These examples show that people in many niches and industries are seeking clarity, support, accountability and direction to help them push past overwhelm and use the information flow to achieve their goals.

Information is worthless if you're not able to use it – and this is where you, the expert entrepreneur, come in.

To build your authority, it's vital to consider how you will create an *outcome* for your market. Over the last ten years, the expert industry has focused too much on delivering information as a commodity, rather than on its use as an outcome. Up until now, selling information has been the easiest way to scale an expert business. But the emphasis is shifting: people don't just want information. It's all out there for them to find for free already. They want an outcome, and they will pay you good money to achieve it. And by helping others to achieve that outcome, your authority will naturally grow.

Outcome-based expert assets

If you want to serve your market effectively, you need to structure your business so that it's an asset that is scalable. To create the reach and impact that influences your market and gives you the freedom to live life on your terms, you need to move beyond focusing on trading time for money. If instead you focus on building assets in your business, you will be able to leverage yourself multiple times without having to worry about building a team. You'll have a business that you can run from wherever you want, whenever you want, while generating income streams that give you a high profit margin.

We are no longer constrained by the traditional rules of business. Office space, full-time staff, utilities and business rates are all liabilities that erode your profit margins and anchor you to a physical location. Your focus should be on committing your resources to building expert assets – your audience, intellectual property and campaigns – so you can operate with a predictable cash flow and plenty of clients. By building assets, developing frameworks and using your own expertise to reach and influence more people, you will build your authority further as your market recognises the unique value you bring. In fact, the biggest asset you will ever design is your framework for how you help others.

Frameworks versus tactics

Frameworks and tactics are different tools. Frameworks provide a set of high-level rules to follow. They are strategic and often stand the test of time, without having to change as the world does. Tactics are ways to follow and use your frameworks. Individual tactics and tools change fairly often; for example, to adapt to innovations in technology.

This book sets out the frameworks I've designed to help people build six-figure profit margin expert businesses. It also includes the tactics that are working now, so you have the tools to do the same. When you create your own framework, it must pass the 'Ronseal test' – it has to do what it says on the tin. Success in this industry is largely about keeping it simple, as the more layers of complexity we build, the more stretched our focus will be.

In terms of tactics, the great news is that over the last couple of years, platforms like Facebook have transformed the face of marketing. We no longer have to build systems based on complex tech to create scarcity (which I refer to as 'manipulation marketing'). Instead, we have moved towards a more authentic way of communicating our message, which creates desire based on our ability to create change.

Right now, most of your competitors don't even realise that this shift has occurred, and they are still using a lot of old-school tactics that are actually *de-positioning* them in front of their markets. When you understand the concept that marketing is now simple and authentic, rather than complex and based on manipulation, building your own authority will become easier and you can rapidly ascend as a major influencer in your niche.

Authority alchemy

When you boil it down, success in business isn't complicated. You need to do two basic things:

1. Build an audience of people you can help

2. Give them an offer that they want

These two steps alone merit separate conversations, and this book covers how to achieve both. But there is a bridge between the two, and you need this critical connection to achieve the results that you deserve.

This step is to build trust with your market through authority and compound it by increasing your intrinsic value: the perception of what you're really worth. Your intrinsic value has a direct impact on what your market will pay to use your services, and you can increase it by building frameworks that de-commoditise your services. Authority and intrinsic value are fundamentally linked and synergistic: raise one, the other follows.

By following a simple set of rules, you can transform the perception your market has of you, directly impacting how you're positioned and what you can charge. This is 'authority alchemy'. Those who miss this piece of the puzzle often fall into the 'tactic trap' instead. After they've created a product, they focus on lead generation and sales rather than audience-building and awareness.

Most of the marketing messages we are exposed to focus on the hacks and tactics of how to get more leads, convert more sales or build better 'funnels'. All these things are desirable, but they are not the rocket fuel that will make your business take off. I've experienced the problem first-hand. When I got started in the industry, I invested in some information products that gave me the marketing templates and emails that the training provider had used in his own business. Using those files, I quickly built a funnel to sell a new digital product I had created. The result when I put my entire database in? Zero sales, and a bucketload of unsubscribes.

The reason the original campaign had worked so well was nothing to do with its structure and copy, but everything to do with the relationship that the expert had already built with his audience.

Ultimately, it doesn't matter what you build. You can have the slickest funnel in the world, the coolest automation and the funkiest Facebook chatbot... but none of it matters if you haven't built up your intrinsic value first. It's like building a Formula One engine and filling it with sludgy diesel that you've siphoned from a tractor.

CASE STUDY – BUILDING AUTHORITY IN FRONT OF A NEW AUDIENCE

JP was my business partner at PEG. When he launched his own consulting business, we started by building out the traditional automation and funnels that had worked for us before, alongside a new information product. We had had such great success at PEG that we thought it would be easy.

When the business launched, it didn't perform as well as either of us had hoped. It was still successful by anyone's book, but it fell short of our expectations. When we went back and analysed the campaign, the issue was obvious. JP had created authority with property investors, but not with letting agents – the audience that he was now serving.

To solve the issue, JP created a Facebook group for letting agents, invited his organic network to give it some momentum, and started to raise his intrinsic value by providing top-level education in the group. We then created a new offer, which was three times more expensive than his first, and launched it through a webinar campaign. The result was £20,000 of sales on launch.

From there, all JP had to do was to continue growing his group and regularly add value to it. The third-party credibility that he had gained through the first intake of his new clients compounded his intrinsic value. These clients became the best ambassadors for JP's programme and continued to accelerate his authority.

Not content with sitting in his comfort zone, JP identified further scope to increase conversion rates, based on the data from the first iteration. We tweaked the offer to communicate an outcome we felt would be more valuable to the audience and ran the webinar again. This time, the webinar created over £50,000 of lifetime customer value sales. This was all from a mailing list of fewer than

1,500 people, a Facebook group with fewer than 1,000 members and JP's organic network.

This change opened my eyes to the power of creating huge value in front of a small but highly relevant and qualified audience. What was really interesting about this process was the minimal resources we needed to achieve the results: the group that JP set up was free. It didn't cost him anything to get people to join, and after making a few tweaks, Facebook began to send more traffic to it for free.

The six-figure expert

One of the attractions of the expert industry is the ability to generate income streams with a high profit margin while leading the lifestyle that works for you. But it is easy to look at the established players who have been building their own businesses for some time, or other niches where the pricing structures are different from yours and feel disillusioned with your progress.

I have yet to discover a niche where you can't generate six-figure profit margins from your home office and with a small team of outsourcers. Whether your sweet spot is high price/low volume or low price/high volume, there's a model that will work for you. Living in a world of instant gratification, we expect to be hitting a six-figure run rate within the first six months of setting up. In reality, there are a few steps that you need to work through.

The first glass ceiling you'll encounter is in the £40,000 to £70,000 bracket of annual sales (note sales, not profit). This is fairly easy to achieve though hustle and diligence alone, but you'll be working long hours to get there – and to sustain it. Even with a healthy 75% profit margin you'll be making less than £50,000 a year. Although that figure might sound good on paper, the process of earning it carries risk and stress. One bad month or a change in circumstances can have enormous consequences.

By putting firmer foundations in place, you will be able to move into the £100,000 to £350,000 turnover bracket (depending on your niche and pricing structure) with minimal support, resources and team members. With the right delivery models and client acquisition systems in place, and if you get the positioning correct, there is little difference in workload up to the top of this bracket.

Summary

The expert industry is going through change. Never have your markets craved more authenticity and transparency from the experts they want to work with, and this creates a huge opportunity for those who understand the fundamental concept that the most important thing to focus on is raising your intrinsic value by building authority.

While everyone else is hunting for the latest 'hack' to short-cut their journey to more leads and sales, you will be quietly building audiences and awareness while creating a business model that's generating high profit margins. You'll have all the ingredients for a business that will reach and influence more people, while generating income streams that will give you freedom and choice.

If you're ready, it's time to look at how you can build those foundations by using the Triple A Method.

CHAPTER TWO

The Triple A Method

The Triple A Method is a framework for rapidly building your authority and leveraging your expertise in today's world. Unlike traditional marketing frameworks, it focuses on providing genuine value and goodwill to your ideal audience through simplicity and 'doing less'. Rather than having to push your audience into action by creating a fear of missing out on a good deal, you want your clients to reach out to you with a deep desire to get the transformational outcome you're offering.

The Pareto principle in reverse

How can we grab the attention of our perfect client in a world where competition is increasing on platforms that have seen a huge decline in organic reach? This is the wrong question to be asking. It's more sensible to ask how we can bypass these shark-infested waters and capture attention in the much larger (and as yet uncontested) blue oceans of your marketplace.

If we analyse any market, we can see the Pareto principle (or the '80/20 rule') in action. Around 20% of the market is currently experiencing a 'pain point', understands what is causing the problem and is already trying to fix it. Depending on the resources available and the complexity of the problem, they may try to fix it themselves, find someone to help them fix it or simply pay someone to make the problem go away.

Some of that 20% will be in your network right now, and they will already know, like and trust you enough to use your services immediately. These people are the 'low-hanging fruit', and for most people in the expert industry they will become their first clients. They might have got to know you at work, on social media, at networking events or through somebody else recommending you. When you launch yourself into your chosen industry, the fact that you've already created demand in the low-hanging fruit in your network can give you the illusion that finding clients is relatively straightforward.

The problem is that you'll run out of low-hanging fruit fairly quickly, forcing you to try to attract clients from the rest of the 20% of your market that is looking for a solution at that time. These people have no idea who you are or what you do, so you have to compete with everyone else who is pitching their services. This 'knife fight in a phone box' inevitably leads to falling prices, as the only thing you can compete on is cost.

Imagine that your ideal client has just realised that she needs the service that you offer. She opens her smartphone, types 'How to do...' into Google and is presented with several million results, all of which are merely a headline of blue text on a white page. The chances that the client will see and click on your entry in the search results at this critical point is close to zero.

The solution is to look at the Pareto principle in a different way: focus your attention on the 80% of the market that is your perfect client but isn't aware of it yet. This means shifting your focus to the long game.

How to play the long game

Human behaviour is highly predictable, so it's possible to anticipate the problems people are going to experience in the next three, six or twelve months and beyond. This is the segment of your audience that you need to focus on. If you develop a relationship with them now, you'll be first to come to mind when they start looking for a solution.

My first training business, PEG, provides an example of this approach.

PEG focused on training property investors in how to systemise and professionalise their businesses. Most businesses go through three main stages: start-up, early stage growth and scaling. Entrepreneurs tend to self-fund their businesses to get going, and then have to put in a lot of hard work to build momentum. This works at first, but it creates problems later because they are trying to grow business with no systems, processes, staff or training in place.

We didn't wait to speak to these business owners until they had run into trouble, working eighty-hour weeks to keep things afloat and seeing their cash flow and profit margins eroding every day. Instead, we created awareness while the entrepreneurs were starting their businesses. When they reached the systemisation stage, we were front of mind: they already knew us, our methods and how we could help them seamlessly achieve their desired outcome.

Creating awareness at an early stage also helps you get better results for your clients. If you take on a client who is already in a place of extreme pain, this makes it harder for them to put your solution in place. In the context of the PEG example above, it can be difficult to systemise your business when you're already working eighty hours a week and struggling to break the cycle.

Another advantage of creating awareness early is that you have more time to build your all-important authority status. In the age of scepticism, authority is something that is earned over time. Although there are many ways to build your intrinsic value and authority faster, there are no shortcuts. You need your market to view you as an authority before they are even thinking about using your services.

Some experts may be tempted to 'hack' the system and create the perception of authority without actually earning it – from 'buying' Likes on social media to making up case studies. Don't give in to this temptation: as social media platforms have become more sophisticated it'll be obvious if you're trying to play the system.

Don't be a busy fool

When creating a client acquisition framework, it's important to consider how to scale it up without having to do a sixty-hour week. A common misconception is that to build authority you need to be writing blogs, recording podcasts, posting five times a day on social media and speaking at every event on the calendar.

All these tactics will help your positioning, but there are smarter ways to get the most out of them without spending your entire life creating content. With appropriate systems and automation, you can easily create an ecosystem that leverages your reach and expertise so that you can consistently bring in new clients and break through your income barrier.

Instead of thinking about the tactics, concentrate on developing a strategy that builds genuine and authentic authority and gets market reach because of the systems you've put in place. This will create an irresistible force of attraction that pulls your ideal clients into your ecosystem. When the time is right, all you have to do is reach out to satisfy their desire to work with you and achieve the transformation you're offering.

Focus on a niche

In any marketplace, the top 20% of businesses tend to dominate over 80% of the revenue share. They do so because they've established themselves as the authority in their space and they've created the momentum and infrastructure to scale their influence to reach wider audiences. When they achieve results for the clients they take on, this increases their authority, which allows them to raise prices and bring on more clients, achieving more results. It's a cycle that quickly increases their market domination.

When JP and I launched PEG, we rapidly grew it to multiple six figures of sales without much of an advertising budget or indeed a team. This success was linked to how we positioned ourselves in front of a tight sub-niche of the property market. Because we decided on this niche early, all our resources went into nurturing a deep but narrow audience. That made it possible to create a consistent and persistent message that reached only the most relevant people.

By reverse-engineering this process and by analysing how other successful expert businesses operated, I created the Triple A Method. One of the best things about this method is you can start using it quickly to build momentum and get results. Building authority doesn't have to take years, because the tools at your disposal today allow you to focus your resources on a small and relevant audience from the start.

Compare this to a competitor who is casting a wide net and spreading themselves thin. They're making a lot of noise, but they're shouting in all directions in the hope that someone will hear. Some people will, of course, but there's no consistency, which makes it difficult for that competitor to grow a sustainable business. In the meantime, you can be quietly attracting and converting the best clients before your competitor is even aware of them.

Three steps to success

The Triple A Method involves three main steps: awareness, authority and automation.

Step 1: Awareness

The first stage is to make your market aware of the real problem that is the cause of the pain they are in. This is called bridging the pain/problem gap. When you bring your market to the point of illumination so that they finally understand their true problem, they will be able to look for solutions. At that point, they need to be aware of your unique process for solving their problem.

Step 2: Authority

Your market is now looking for a solution provider and they are aware of how you can help. If you haven't already established yourself as an authority, they simply won't trust you enough to become your clients. To build your authority, you need to raise your intrinsic value through demonstration, association and education. To magnify that authority, you need to be consistent.

Step 3: Automation

This final step is all about systems. When you get started in your business, especially if you're bootstrapping it, you'll have to spend some time in 'hustle' mode, roll your sleeves up and work hard to gain momentum. To accelerate that momentum, though, you need the right systems in place to grow. That involves automating your audience creation, attraction and ascension.

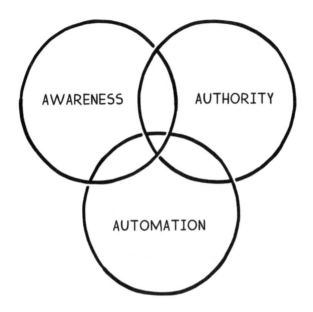

Figure 2.1 Awareness–Authority–Automation model

You need to have all three elements working for the method to truly effective:

- If you've established awareness and authority but you have no automation, you will hit a glass ceiling of organic growth and get stuck in the 'time for money' trap. You have no scalability.

- If you've established authority and created automation but you haven't built awareness, your market won't know they have a problem that you can solve. Even if you're the best at what you do, you'll be off their radar.

- Finally, if you've created awareness and automation but you haven't built your authority, your market will not trust you. You could be an exceptional entrepreneur who can genuinely help people, but your market doesn't regard you as such.

When you've achieved all three steps, you'll amplify your delivery model. This is where you need to be careful: if you're amplifying a delivery model that hasn't been optimised for scale and profit, you will be amplifying a liability.

Delivery models are often brushed over in the wider context of growing an expert business. This is dangerous, as an expert entrepreneur must be able to not only provide a service that's fit for purpose and gets results for their clients, but also deliver it effectively. I've seen expert entrepreneurs create a product, make lots of sales but then struggle with the delivery, leading to massive refunds and destroying any goodwill they had in the market.

If you get the delivery model right, this will have a big impact on building your authority.

Summary

In this chapter we've looked at the importance of playing the long game and building up your authority in front of a very defined niche. I developed the Triple A Method to help you do this, which we'll break down in detail over the next four chapters.

Let's dive into it.

CHAPTER THREE

Awareness

Have you ever logged on to LinkedIn and felt frustrated or angry about the number of cold pitches you find in your mailbox? We're bombarded with so many that they become one annoying hiss of background noise. We find this so jarring because we have no idea who the person is and, more fundamentally, we're not even aware that we have a problem that they can solve. If your market doesn't understand that they have a problem you can solve, they won't be looking for a solution. You could be the best in the world at what you do, but your offers are immediately disregarded.

On the other hand, every now and then someone approaches us with an offer that resonates as something we need. We might wonder how this individual knows us so well that they seem to fully understand the problem we are facing and be offering the perfect solution. Either this person has got lucky by playing the volume game, or they've already built our awareness without us even realising.

With that in mind, the first thing you need to do is build awareness in your market about the real problems they have and how you can solve them. The awareness-raising stage is made up of three elements: pain, problem and process.

Pain

Regardless of who we are, what stage our business is at or the success we've had, most of us feel some sort of pain in our lives – often, every day. This pain sits on a spectrum from 'slight background annoyance' to 'severely acute'.

In business, the main types of pain are:

- Lack of money (or cash flow)
- Lack of time
- Lack of wellbeing (for example, health problems, relationship difficulties)

Often, just one of these pain points will spill over into one or both of the others. For example, as expert entrepreneurs, we tend to bootstrap our businesses through the start-up phase, which means we're often away from home, trying to get to as many networking meetings as possible and have as many 'cups of coffee' with people who we've briefly met online. That creates pain in our lives.

When I was getting started as a stage speaker in 2014, I was spending all my free time trying to get invited on to as many stages as possible to sell my first property workshop. Getting to and from networking meetings often meant travelling for hours through the middle of the night, more than once a week. One of the issues with this tactic was that the audience I was speaking to had no awareness of the problem I was solving. This would often lead to no sales at all, the feeling of failure and the fear that I was on the wrong path. I couldn't understand it – I had sat in plenty of rooms myself and seen people running to enrol on a programme or mentorship afterwards.

This led to some pain points – a lack of money and lack of time – that started to affect me every day. It's no surprise that when you put these two pain points together, they can affect the relationships around you and lead to the third pain point. My wife was always supportive, but if you're away several times a week, come back empty handed (save the hotel bills and fuel receipts) and leave your partner to deal with your two young children, things can be affected.

To some extent, these pain points will always exist in some form. Those who are getting started with their business are likely to feel the lack of cash flow. Those who have built a team and are scaling their business are likely to have compressed margins, leading to worries about having enough money to pay everyone at the end of the month. And those who are earning big profits are still likely to worry about how to protect, invest and compound that wealth.

This means that every niche you can think of will experience some form of pain point, whether it's simmering in the background or keeping them up at night. It is important, therefore, to be clear about what your niche is so you can accurately identify the pain points in the awareness process. There's no point in talking about bootstrapping a start-up if your niche is high-growth companies that are looking to scale.

Here's the leap that most expert entrepreneurs miss when they start to market their services: the pain that someone feels is the effect, not the cause. It is merely the manifestation of the real problem that someone has in their life or business. Until they understand what their real problem is, they're unlikely to look for a solution.

Where that pain is on the spectrum is important here. If it's a dull ache, it hasn't got to the point where it's so painful that we take action to fix it. As humans, we generally like to ignore things until it's too late. At the other end of the spectrum, the pain is so acute that we lose the ability to make rational decisions, and we start making bad ones. As an expert, you need to ensure that you help people in your market before they get to this stage.

Problem

As an expert, your job is to remove your potential clients' pain points, but to do so you must first identify and solve the real problem they are facing. A fundamental part of the awareness process is to bring your audience to the 'point of illumination'. This is the lightbulb moment – the point when they realise what the real problem is that they need to solve. When your audience reaches that point, they start to seek a solution.

If your audience reaches the point of illumination before they're aware of you and what you can do to help, they'll already be checking out your competitors and looking for the best deal on offer. This is why there's so much noise in most of the markets as an increasing amount of service providers try to capture the attention of the small percentage of a market that is actively looking for a solution.

If we bring someone to the point of illumination ourselves, when that person starts to look for a solution it follows that you will be at the front of their mind. One of the keys to the awareness-building process is, therefore, to bridge the pain/problem gap.

Here are some examples from the expert industry:

Pain	Real problem
Lack of time, always feeling like you're hustling	Running too many business models or delivery models
	Running delivery models where you are trading your time for money
	Not having the right systems in place to run the business smoothly
Lack of customers	Inconsistent and unpredictable lead generation – 'feast or famine'
	No follow-up systems, despite meeting plenty of prospects
	Poor sales process
Lack of profit	Incorrect pricing structure – trading time for money at a rate doesn't create enough profit
	Lack of authority – unable to command premium pricing
	Inflated overheads
Fear of failure, lack of self-belief	Lack of clarity around purpose, vision and goals
	Lack of knowledge about processes

It's important to spend some time identifying the pain that your niche faces. It's important to understand this, because everything from this point on is based on this foundation.

When you understand the real problem your market faces, the next thing you need to do is tell them how you solve it.

Process

So far, we've focused on creating awareness in your market. Now you need to bring the attention back to yourself and identify the process you will use to solve the market's problem. At this stage, and to some extent throughout your client acquisition lifecycle, your market really doesn't care much about you. Your ideal clients may resonate with you and your values, but ultimately they care about the outcome you create: what's in it for them.

That means you need to differentiate yourself from your competition to make sure you can compete on more than price alone. The quickest and easiest way of achieving this is to design a unique process, methodology or framework for how you solve your market's problems. This has three main effects:

- It de-commoditises you and sets you apart from your competitors.

- It makes your methods easier to remember and understand. People receive hundreds of marketing messages every day, so the simple ones are the ones that stick in the mind.

- It rapidly increases your intrinsic value and positions you as an authority, leading to more demand and the ability to command higher prices.

Your process – or your methodology – is different from your product or service. When I work on this with my clients, initially they often default to explaining what they do in relation to their programme or product. Think about it like this: your process should be a framework that you can use to create multiple products, programmes or services. Your services are there to teach or deliver your process.

CASE STUDY – DEVELOPING A UNIQUE PROCESS

Kieron, a client on my core programme, the Authority Accelerator, is an exceptional copywriter. He provides this service predominantly as part of a team that works with larger agencies. This is a familiar story for service providers who want to move from being a freelancer to owning an agency themselves, allowing them to command higher rates. Kieron approached me because he wanted to set up his own client acquisition systems and develop training for other entrepreneurs on how to write effective copy.

When I asked him what his unique process was, his initial answer was:

- Step 1 – Hold an initial strategy and messaging session
- Step 2 – Host a one-day workshop to uncover the unique value proposition
- Step 3 – Create the first round of copy
- Step 4 – Host a second one-day workshop to refine the message
- Step 5 – Refine and create the second round of copy

Kieron had set out a delivery process, rather than a unique framework that communicates why what he does is more valuable than what his competitors do. After breaking down how and why Kieron writes his copy, we designed his own process – the CATCH system:

- **C**haracter – Defining your tone of voice, brand and visual identity
- **A**mbition – What are your mission, purpose, business aims and objectives?
- **T**ransformation – What transformation will you deliver for your customer and how do you communicate that?

- **C**ompetition – Understanding how to stand out in your space against your competitors
- **H**ow – Your own business process, what you have done before, case studies, proof and statistics

This CATCH system is easy to communicate, unique, and doesn't mention writing copy once! Kieron isn't just a 'copywriter' anymore; he's much more than that. He can communicate his ability to deeply understand you, your market and how to attract a consistent flow of leads. This is often the case when people spend some time reflecting deeply on what they actually do.

As we designed this framework together, I arrived at my own point of illumination: I needed a better copywriter! I didn't have to look far, as I was already aware of the process that would solve my problem and hired Kieron on the spot.

This case study shows that everyone, regardless of their background, experience or success, has bigger problems to solve and needs solution providers – but no one likes to be pitched to. If Kieron had sent me an email to offer his services, I would almost certainly have rejected him: we put up strong defences when unsolicited advances arrive. But when you present an irresistible outcome to someone who's just become aware of the real problem they face, you'll attract more business than you can handle.

How to design a strong framework

Designing your unique framework will bring you some of the highest returns on effort in your expert business. Doing this takes hours and minutes, not weeks and days, and you can refine it over time. Once you've created your framework, you will have an asset that will bring returns for years to come.

Here are my rules for designing your framework:

1. **Make it outcome based.** Your framework must communicate the outcome it creates for your marketplace. To do this effectively, you need to understand the problem they need to overcome (Point A) and where they are trying to get to by solving the problem (Point B). This is the 'pain to gain' journey. By setting this out, your market will find it easier to visualise the outcome you are providing for them, which creates demand for your services.

2. **Keep it simple.** Entrepreneurs tend to over-complicate things. You should be able to get on stage with a blank flip chart and marker pen and explain your process to the audience in no more than sixty seconds. Anything more creates confusion and overwhelm.

3. **Make it visual.** People retain information more easily when it's delivered visually: a picture paints a thousand words.

I use three main visual frameworks: linear, cyclical and layered.

Linear frameworks

The simplest model you can use is the linear 'straight line from A to B'. You walk your client through a series of steps that will get them from A to B. This model is suitable when you have a defined process and outcome, and you can break each step down into its own linear model.

Let's say you're helping someone in the expert industry move from the five-figure hamster wheel to a leveraged, six-figure profit margin business. There is a tried and tested framework to follow:

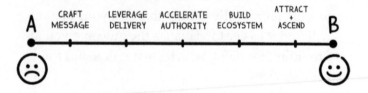

Figure 3.1 Linear 'A to B' framework

- Step 1: create models and message

- Step 2: redesign service delivery for leverage and profit

- Step 3: position as authority

- Step 4: build value ecosystem

- Step 5: attract and ascend relevant audiences

With this linear model, there's only one route. You're not going to start by trying to attract your audiences if you haven't built the systems to capture and ascend them, or if you haven't got a delivery model that you can scale. It also shows how powerful it is to have a framework that helps you communicate outcomes rather than saying, for example, 'Let's get some Facebook ads running and see what happens'.

Cyclical frameworks

The second visual model depicts a process that keeps evolving. Essentially, it's a linear model that's wrapped around to meet itself at the start. Here's an example of the process we used in PEG:

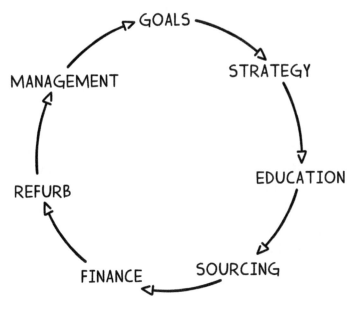

Figure 3.2 The cyclical framework

The cyclical model conveys the impression of constant growth. This is more effective on a strategic level, and the linear model is more effective on a tactical level (when someone needs to achieve one outcome, quickly).

Layered frameworks

The layered framework is the one that is used for the Triple A Method, and it can be applied to many different niches. In business and in life, the route to a result is rarely a straight line. The layered framework can be used to explain how various areas overlap and link together, using a visual model that is easy to understand.

Here's an example of the Quantum Method, which my client Ross created to help busy professionals get back into flow and achieve balance in life. It covers the three main pillars of wealth, health and mindset and explains how we, as humans, need to be in balance to achieve a true state of high performance.

The layered framework works well when there is no precise starting point and when you need to tailor your process to the client. In Ross's example, you would need to address wealth, health and mindset in synergy, but one of the three may be more urgent and addressing it may lead to quicker wins.

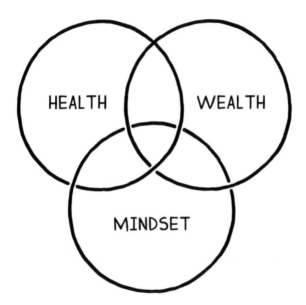

Figure 3.3 The layered framework

The layered framework is useful for strategic models that convey your concepts at a high level. You can then use linear frameworks to help execute the tactics that you teach.

Summary

This chapter has outlined the importance of creating awareness in your market. By doing so, you will bring your potential clients from a state of feeling pain to the point of illumination, where they understand their real problem and start looking for a solution. Once you have bridged that gap, you need to ensure that they are aware of your unique process for solving their problem. By offering a transformational outcome, your unique process will raise your intrinsic value.

CHAPTER THREE: EXERCISES

Answering the following questions will help you to define your market's problems and how you can help solve them.

1. What is my market's pain points? Think about what keeps them up at night screaming at the ceiling! Pain points will generally fall into some degree of a lack of time, a lack of money or a conflict in a relationship.

2. What are the real problems they have? After you've defined your market's pain points, which are the effect, work it backwards to define the cause which is their ultimate problem. For example, if someone's pain is lack of time because they're always on the road finding clients, the real problem maybe that they don't have a predictable and consistent lead generation system in place.

3. What is my process (framework) to solve the problems? This is your unique method to take people from 'Point A' (where they are unhappy) to 'Point B' (where they are happy).

CHAPTER FOUR

Authority

One factor differentiates the 5% of expert entrepreneurs who dominate over 80% of the market from everyone else. That's *authority*.

It is *not* the ability to spend the most on adverts, write the best copy, have the best products, command the biggest teams, employ the most cut-throat salespeople, develop the coolest funnels or deploy the latest chatbots. These things will all help increase your conversion rates along the way, but if your market does not trust you, they will not buy. The key to becoming the most sought-after solution in your market is to accelerate your authority and raise your intrinsic value in that market.

Experts who grasp this concept quickly will get an immediate advantage over their competitors, because building authority is one of the most straightforward ways to build a business that truly makes a difference. It's certainly simpler than building funnels, mastering Facebook ads, writing copy or grappling with tech. But simple is not always easy, and the biggest barrier that's standing between where you are now and where you want to be is you.

Most of the clients I work with know how to coach, train or serve. Put them in a room with their own clients and they're in flow. The barrier lies in pushing yourself out of your comfort zone, putting your head above the parapet and building your visibility, value and authority. Most of us have some form of fear that's preventing us from taking action to achieve this, but if you can overcome that fear and take decisive action you will see immediate results.

This chapter looks at the methods you should be using to accelerate your authority. These are the pillars of demonstration, association and education. Think of it as follows:

$$Authority = (D + A + E) \times C$$

The 'C' stands for *consistency*. In a world of ever-increasing information flow, where we are bombarded with daily marketing messages, to get noticed and build your authority you need to project your message consistently. Otherwise, it will quickly be forgotten. You might be thinking, 'I don't have anything to post regularly' or 'I don't have the time to post regularly' – but in the new era of social media, you can use a system that will do it for you. You can easily set up your systems to distribute powerful content to the right person, at the right time, with merely a few clicks of a mouse.

We will return to consistency later. For now, let's focus on what we need to do to build our authority in the first place.

Demonstration

The first step to building your own authority is to show who you are and what you do. Humans have tribal traits, so we tend to stick in groups that share our own values and belief systems. On the spectrum of values, most people are somewhere in the middle.

Value matching

To be able to demonstrate our values, we need to first understand them. We also need to understand the value that our market has.

For example, I strongly stand for promoting authenticity and transparency in the expert industry. Therefore, I stand against using manipulation and scarcity to make sales. I believe that we should never lie to or be disingenuous with our markets; otherwise, our clients will sign up because of a fear of missing out rather than a true desire to work with us to achieve the transformation that we offer. These are the values that I would project into the marketplace. By doing so, I will attract those who resonate with this message and repel those who would rather use different methods.

There is no definitive right or wrong; it is simply a demonstration of personal values. The more you demonstrate your values, and the further on each side of the spectrum they lie, the more you will divide your audience, repelling some while building a deep bond with others.

The very mention of the word 'repel' makes some experts feel nervous about abuse being hurled at them, so they try to appeal to the whole market. Inevitably, this waters down your message and ultimately does not appeal to anyone – you'll blend in with the crowd rather than capturing attention. That doesn't mean that you should sit at one extreme or the other and make up a value set that you *think* your market wants you to demonstrate. This is disingenuous, and you'll be caught out at some point. It means that you need to develop a deeper level of self-awareness, understand your unique and authentic set of values and beliefs, and have the courage and conviction to demonstrate them to your market and stand by them, even when it feels that others don't agree.

To gain awareness of how your actions demonstrate your values, ask yourself these questions:

- What image of yourself do you present – on social media for example?

- What clothes do you wear?

- What language do you use when you write or create videos?

- What tokens do you surround yourself with? For example, what car do you drive? What watch do you wear?

- What personal brand do you exude?

The image of someone in full hustle mode, working hard and playing hard surrounded by expensive watches, supercars and luxury projects is very different from that of a family man, focusing on systems, balance and a different pace of life. Neither is right or wrong, but both will attract different audiences. This is why you *must* be fully aware of the values you are projecting: you will attract people with the same value set. If you create an image that you *think* your market wants to see, you will often attract clients who jar with your true value set. That will create conflict in your relationship.

Association

Who you are seen to associate with has one of the strongest impacts on your own authority. This 'third-party association' is a powerful tool because the message that is demonstrated is not created by you, which gives it much more credibility with your audience.

In the world of social media, it's easy to create a reality that doesn't exist. Anyone can hire a supercar for the day, airbrush pictures of themselves and present an image that isn't true. With business models like AirBnB being rolled out into other industries, luxuries like access to private aviation have never been more accessible. There is nothing like a few selfies in a private jet splashed around Facebook to paint a picture of success, even if you never got airborne.

Audiences are rapidly becoming savvier and more sophisticated, and most people will quickly see through the private jet pictures or the 100,000 Facebook followers you've bought who don't engage on your page at all. But when you demonstrate that third-party association, your market is compelled to believe that this perception is reality, and authority is automatically bestowed on you.

There are two types of association we can leverage: association with celebrity and association with results.

Association with celebrity

When I say celebrity, I don't mean a Hollywood A lister. I mean the few individuals in your industry who are already viewed as authorities and influencers in their own right. Associating with these people will see their authority transfer to you.

We live in a culture that is obsessed with celebrity and being associated with the 'celebrities' in our industry skyrockets our own worth. Consider the effect that reality TV has on ordinary members of the public who appear on it.

There are some rules to follow to get this right:

- **Make sure your values align with those of the celebrity.** On one occasion I was interviewing another high-profile property developer for an episode of PEG TV, our authority-building content. After the episode aired, several people contacted me to ask why I had done the interview, as the individual didn't gel with my own values. This mismatch had caused an issue with my target audience. This highlights the importance of value matching.

- **Position yourself correctly alongside the celebrity.** You want to appear on an equal footing in the relationship. This means finding a balance between your needs and theirs. Grabbing a quick selfie at an event is great, but most will see that there's no substance to it. Interviewing an influencer is always a strong method of association, as is sharing a stage with them at an event (either someone else's or your own). Partnering with them on a product, event or service will rapidly see that transference of authority.

- **Work in synergy with the celebrity, not in competition.** It goes without saying that there has to be something in it for them. You're not likely to be able to send them a quick message on Facebook and instantly have an industry influencer on board, working to raise your status. Always think about what you can offer them of value. The synergy of cross-pollinating audiences will benefit both of you, assuming you have an audience to start with. If you don't, you may have to start lower on the 'celebrity scale'. You can opt to pay your chosen celebrity to endorse your product or service in the first instance – as long as this is clear to your audience. As your own authority, audience and value grows, you will be able to move up the scale in terms of who will associate with you.

Association with results

Association with celebrity will give your authority a 'shot in the arm' for the short term, but it lacks tangible substance and long-term effect. To solve this problem, you need to associate yourself with the outcome you create for others.

Remember, your market only cares about what you can do for *them*. The most effective way to communicate this is to show the results that you have achieved for your clients in the past. Testimonials and case studies help internalise the trust that you can do what you claim to be able to do, giving you the ultimate credibility.

As you work with more clients and get results, you should always document their success and strive to receive testimonials and case studies. A case study is always more effective than a testimonial, because it demonstrates the outcome and how it was achieved. All too often, the only social proof an expert entrepreneur can get their hands on is a quick interview with a workshop delegate, who enthuses about how great the content was, the buzz and energy in the room, and maybe even the quality of the venue and the refreshments. These kind words are certainly better than nothing, but they don't convey that all-important outcome and your ability to create results.

Compare that with a case study, like the following one:

CASE STUDY – DEMONSTRATING OUTCOMES

David joined my Authority Accelerator programme because he wanted to get his mentoring programme off the ground in the property industry. David had already launched his one-to-one mentoring service, and he was publishing a lot of free content, which was encouraging people to connect with him. The problem was the next step in the ascension process: the all-important conversion from lead to mentee. David found that he was spending a lot of time speaking to people on the phone, delivering more and more value, but they weren't signing up to his programme.

When we analysed what was going on, we identified these issues:

1. **David's mentoring programme was not outcome-based.** That meant that his leads were not sure of what they were being offered. This can often be an issue with mentoring and accountability, because it's difficult to visualise the steps to achieving the outcome.

2. **David didn't have a unique process to achieve the outcomes.** That compounded the first issue, making it more difficult for his leads to visualise how an outcome would be achieved. Not having a unique process also meant that David couldn't increase his intrinsic value.

3. **David had a conversion rate of zero from ten phone calls.** His strategy was simple: to impress the leads with extra value, helping them as much as possible before discussing his mentoring programme. This strategy rarely works when you're trying to encourage a lead to buy into a programme rather than a one-off service – a high-ticket programme – because you are effectively coaching them with their problem rather than bringing them to the conclusion that they want to work with you to understand what the problem actually is and solve it.

Here's what we did to solve these issues:

1. **We created a unique framework that identified the market's real problems.** The problem was that serviced accommodation businesses lacked systemisation at the early stage of growth, which led to the market becoming stuck in hustle, overwhelm and burnout. We created the SOS Method, which communicated David's process for creating a scalable business.

2. **We pivoted the delivery model.** Instead of starting with a one-to-one mentoring programme, we created a ninety-day group coaching programme that walked trainees through the steps in the SOS Method. Because it was a group programme, David could lower the barrier to entry by reducing the cost. He could

also give his leads a tangible outcome that they could achieve in a realistic time frame.

3. **We created a process for the consultation calls.** I gave David a tried and tested framework for conducting consultation calls with leads in a way that brings a lead to the point of sale without having to be 'salesy'. Many experts, after doing all the hard work to get someone on the phone, fail to get a result because they 'just want to help' and are embarrassed to ask for the sale. The framework we used bypasses all that awkwardness and means you never have to make cringeworthy offers again!

Putting this in place took just three weeks. In week four of the Authority Accelerator, David carried out my 'beta tester launch' sequence. Using social media tactics, he told his organic audiences what he was doing. The aim was to get immediate feedback for his new offer and, hopefully, some sales.

David brought on his first three clients from just three calls – a 100% conversion rate – and paid back his entire investment in the Authority Accelerator. In the next few days, he had filled his first group coaching programme and earned £18,000 in sales.

Education

The final pillar of authority is to educate your market. The process of education leads to some powerful psychological drivers:

- **Reciprocity.** When you teach using your knowledge and experience, you're harnessing one of the most powerful influence triggers you can: the law of reciprocity. The law is simple: the value that you give to the world will be returned to you with a high rate of interest.

- **Perception.** When we educate, we are perceived in a different light. Most businesses engage in marketing and sales to sell their services. There is nothing wrong with this, but people will see you as a salesperson. When we educate, we are regarded as a teacher. And educators – teachers, professors, lecturers – are regarded as authorities in their area. As we become seen as an authority, people in our market lose their inherent scepticism about our motives and allow our messaging to enter their minds.

Never use this technique to manipulate your market. You're here to promote action in your market and get results, not to flog a load of rubbish to people who can never use it. If you use it to grow your authority and reach more people with a genuinely positive impact, the sales and profits will follow.

When putting out educational content, there are some rules to follow.

Rule 1: Cater for different learning styles

People in your market will have different learning styles, so distribute your content using multiple formats. Some people would rather watch a video, some would rather read an article, and some would prefer to listen to a podcast. As you create more content, you will find which style works for you; that will become your core style. You can then ripple the content across other platforms and repurpose it for other mediums.

Here's an example of how you can repurpose content. Imagine shooting a five-minute video on your smartphone and immediately uploading it to social media. You can then send the video to be transcribed (some companies, such as www.rev.com charge from $1 a minute of video). That gives you a transcript that you can post as an article. You could separate the audio and share it as a podcast. You could even take the article, split it into micro content, extract some quotes and create an infographic from it. This makes it much easier to share content regularly.

Rule 2: Keep it relevant

Your educational content needs to be relevant to your market and how you help them. It also needs to seamlessly take the consumer deeper into your ecosystem. It may be tempting to get content out for content's sake, but if it is not relevant then it will be ignored or even confuse the message you're trying to get across. We'll look at the core pillars of messaging in Chapter Seven.

Rule 3: Keep it at a high level

Pitch your free content at a high level, focusing on frameworks and concepts rather than technical training. It can be easy to overwhelm an audience with technical content if they are only just getting to know you; you can introduce deeper level content later in the process. That said, it's important to teach your best content for free: in the current market, information is worthless if it isn't used correctly. Don't be afraid to give a lot of value, as your results will be directly proportional – people will still need your help to be able to act on the information you're teaching them.

Rule 4: Be consistent

You need to deliver educational content consistently. Most social media platforms have a 'decay' feature built into their distribution algorithm, which means that anything you post will have a shelf life of visibility. Also, people have instant access to a ready supply of media that is probably more entertaining than yours. In this environment your content will be quickly forgotten, even if it does resonate with the consumer.

By creating a regular 'content spot', you can hold yourself to account to consistently release educational content to the market. Traditional media is quickly being replaced by on-demand media (think of terrestrial TV versus Netflix), so you need to operate as your own 'edu-tainment' channel, regularly releasing on-demand content. That gives the viewer the option to binge on all your previous content, rapidly increasing trust and intrinsic value.

If it is not there, or people can't find it, they'll inevitably drop into one of your competitors' spheres of influence.

Summary

This chapter has looked at the fundamental differences between the experts who dominate their marketplace, and everyone else: they build authority and they add to their intrinsic value. Many people struggle to build their own authority because they don't want to raise their head above the parapet and leave themselves open to comment and criticism. This fear never goes away, but the more you stay true to your unique values, the more effectively you learn to deal with the division this creates. After you've pushed through those fears, you can rapidly build your own authority through demonstration, association and education – all of which are compounded by consistency.

CHAPTER 4: EXERCISES

As discussed in this chapter, to be able to demonstrate our values, we need to first understand them. We also need to understand the value that our market has.

1. To define your own values, write down what you desire, what you fear, what you stand for and what you stand against. You can use the following as prompts if it's helpful:

   – Desires (eg financial freedom, travel, autonomy)

   – Fears (eg recession, lack of cash-flow, rejection)

   – Stand for (eg authenticity, transparency)

   – Stand against (eg scarcity, manipulation)

2. Repeat this exercise for your target market – match the common values. These are the values that you should demonstrate in everything you put out into the public space.

3. Association

   Brainstorm the existing influencers in your industry. Ask the following questions:

   i. Is there synergy or competition between you?

   ii. Do they have an engaged audience/list?

    iii. Are they approachable to opportunities?
       If you think there is scope for partnership, connect with them and develop a relationship **before** discussing partnership opportunities.

4. Education

What regular content slot can I produce?
Create a theme for this (eg property investment, mindset and motivation, lead generation, systems) and look to create two to four pieces of content per month.

Different mediums are:

    i.   Blog

    ii. Vlog

    iii. Video 'channel'

    iv. Podcast

    v. Physical newsletter

CHAPTER FIVE

Automation

If you're just getting started or you're stuck on the 'time for money' hamster wheel, you first need to gain momentum in front of your existing audience. You've probably spent your entire life unconsciously creating networks across communities – on social media, at networking events, in professional associations and in your social life. Every time you connect with someone, regardless of the level, an invisible bond is formed. That bond is like a web of tendrils, and you never know when someone is going to pull on one of them.

You can gain momentum from this existing audience. Having created these connections, you've already started the 'know, like, trust' process and (hopefully) established some intrinsic value. To build a business that can reach and influence – and ultimately profit – on a much larger scale, the next step is to build systems that will facilitate that 'know, like, trust' process. I recommend bringing in automation as quickly as you can.

For the five-figure expert, the traditional cycle is one of feast and famine. You focus on making sales to your network. You hit the networking circuit, post regularly on social media and ask as many people as you can for referrals. If it all goes to plan, you will make some sales. But then you need to switch to delivery mode. While you're delivering, you don't have the time or energy to be marketing and selling, so the pipeline runs dry. You deliver during the day and hustle during the evenings, but you're having to work harder and harder to maintain your income, and you start to burn out. Sales drop off, clients end their time with you, and you have to start the whole process again.

Imagine that instead, you can sit back and relax with the knowledge and confidence that your systems are working for you, bringing in a steady flow of leads and converting them into paying clients. This security frees you up, financially and mentally, to focus on the things that really matter: delivering value, serving your clients and achieving balance in your life. You have control and freedom of choice.

To achieve this, it's crucial to use systems and automation that will allow you to grow.

The new world of simplicity

In my experience, what prevents many people from moving from a five- to a six-figure income is the misconception that you need to be a tech wizard to automate your business.

A few years ago, this was a valid argument: you needed a high level of technical ability to use most of the software platforms, website content management systems and page builders, customer relationship management systems and autoresponders. Glossy websites and intricate funnels were the domain of those with technical expertise and those who could afford to pay for that expertise. This created a barrier for the bootstrapping expert entrepreneur. If you're working sixty hours a week just to bring on your first clients, you can't afford to hire a team of web designers, copywriters and advertising specialists to build out your ecosystems.

Today, technology has never been simpler to use. There has been an explosion in software as a service (SaaS) platforms, which are designed with the end user in mind. Fierce competition among the main players means that these platforms are becoming ever more user-friendly, and the prices are becoming more competitive. Now it's as simple as 'drag and drop'. In a matter of hours, with just a mobile phone and a Facebook account, you can build a powerful attraction system that costs you pennies to bring in high-quality leads.

You can automate three main areas that will free you up to focus on adding value, rather than getting bogged down with operations:

1. **Audiences:** Creating a defined group of people who we can build relationships with over time

2. **Attraction:** Bringing a predictable and consistent flow of leads into our audience

3. **Ascension:** Taking our audience through a process that adds value while converting them into customers

Audiences

An audience is a defined group of people who you can communicate with. When email became mainstream, it revolutionised marketing by giving us the ability to communicate quickly with people on a list. That was the first real online audience that we could build.

Email is still a brilliant way to do business with your audience. It is still viewed as a medium through which to make transactions and offer services, so you're less likely to break rapport when you do make offers. As mentioned earlier, however, we've seen a decline in email open rates over the years, as the number of marketing emails people receive every day has grown. Increasingly sophisticated filtering systems in email servers are stopping marketing emails getting into our inbox in the first place, and new regulations, such as the General Data Protection Regulation (GDPR), have added additional steps to capture and market to an email address. It's no surprise that open rates and click-through rates are declining.

Fortunately, we now have many other ways of building audiences in the modern world, and all of them are highly automatable. It is crucial to build an *audience*, not just a list. An audience is a group of people who resonate with your values and messaging and have engaged with you at some point. Your systems will know when this engagement has happened and automatically place the individual in your audience so you can continue to build a relationship. This is fundamentally different from the old way of building a list of people and then selling them stuff.

Building audiences that are based on engagement has a twofold effect on your business.

1. **It's an effective filtering system.** When you put content out to the world, no matter how much you have tried to target it, it will find its way to people who are not relevant to you or your services. That's fine; not everyone in the world is your perfect customer. But by capturing interest based on engagement, you can create a much more refined group of people to communicate with.

2. **It allows you to focus your efforts.** Once you
   have a filtering system in place, you can focus all
   your efforts and resources on communicating a
   consistent message to this much smaller group of
   people. This makes your process more effective
   in terms of conversion rates and, importantly,
   cost. Driving down the cost of acquiring a client
   gives you a big advantage over your competitors,
   because you can increase your margins, re-invest
   your profits and gain momentum in your market.

Here's how powerful this is in practice. You can pick
up a phone and a selfie stick, shoot a five-minute
Facebook Live video with some educational content,
and then automatically include anyone who watches a
percentage of that video into an audience that you can
communicate with whenever you want. You can do this
for pennies on the pound compared with traditional
ways of generating leads.

Right now, the rewards we get for using the marketing
resources available to us are much greater than the
costs. For example, one of my clients recently launched
a campaign where he shared a series of five-minute videos that he had made himself. His automated system
dropped everyone who watched them into a Facebook
audience. He then paid to place a 'call to action' advert
in front of everyone who saw more than 25% of any
of his videos. When we analysed the campaign on
one of my Inner Circle sessions, we found that he was
booking consultation calls in at less than £15 a call. The

programme that he is selling on those calls is priced at £1,500, which is great value for those who take part in it. To make just a small profit on this campaign, he has to convert just one call out of every 100 made. Even at a 10% conversion rate, he would be spending £150 on adverts to make a £1,500 sale – ten times the cost of the 'ad spend'.

This is audience-building with pinpoint accuracy. Later, we'll look at a toolkit of resources that you can use and update to build your own audiences. What's important at this point is to understand that your focus needs to be on creating and growing a relationship with a small but highly engaged audience. That will be the most valuable asset you will have in your business.

Attraction

Before you can build your audience, you need to set up the attraction systems that will bring the right people into it.

In general, experts who are stuck in the 'time for money' trap use three common methods to attract clients:

1. Networking events

2. Organic social media

3. Referrals

All these techniques work, and they will bring you clients. You've spent years building up your existing organic networks, and you can build momentum there for immediate results.

The problem with these techniques is that they're not consistent or predictable. They involve you either investing a lot of effort in outbound lead generation or having to pay referral partners for the business they generate. A coach I spoke to at a strategy day I hosted told me that most of his clients came through an agency that took more than 50% of his revenues. That's a lot of profit being left on the table.

Without predictability in your lead generation, it's impossible to scale to six figures because you can't plan your cash flow when you don't know what's coming in every month. When you've refined your systems, you'll have a set of metrics that will give you the confidence that when you put £1,000 of advertising spend into a campaign, you'll get £2,000 back within a certain period.

Paid-for lead generation

Almost all business owners know they should be consistently generating new leads, but they hesitate to pay for them. In my experience, there's a lot of fear, uncertainty and doubt surrounding paid-for lead generation, but it's actually the least risky and most leverageable way of growing your business. This uncertainty is partly caused by the rapid rate at which social media platforms are making changes to improve their systems. These changes can make us feel overwhelmed, but in reality, they are usually superficial or ergonomic; the fundamental methods you would use to run Facebook ads have not changed in years.

Every now and again, though, platforms do roll out a major update, which panics everyone and spreads a ripple of misinformation around the community. At the start of 2018, for example, Facebook announced a major change to its algorithm. That change throttled organic reach for personal and business profiles. A copy-and-paste post was being shared, warning you that Facebook would now limit your reach to only six people, and you had no control over who they would be. This was nonsense, but some feared that it meant the end of Facebook as a relevant advertising platform for businesses. Many big influencers who had built organic audiences were upset by the change and decided to publicly take their audiences to other platforms as a matter of principle. But the update did not affect the ad platform at all. In fact, it made it even more important for businesses to understand how to get the most out of the power of paid-for ads. For me and for my 'where I manage their marketing', the result was actually a *drop* in average cost per lead over 2018.

Another issue that causes people to shy away from paid-for advertising is 'pub talk' syndrome. You've spoken to someone who chatted with a mate in the pub who said that he put a load of cash into a Facebook ad once and didn't get any return. All of a sudden, a chat over a pint equates to the false paradigm that the Facebook ad platform doesn't work. The reality is more complex. Many people 'dabble' with paid-for advertising, put in a chunk of money in a short space of time without understanding the platform, and then wonder why it all falls through.

Another reason people don't invest in paid-for advertising is that they see it as a business cost, rather than an investment that creates a return. If I told you to put £1,000 into a Facebook ad campaign, your default thought process might be that you'll never see that £1,000 again. However, if you had built a system where for every £1,000 you put into ad spend, you knew that you were likely to get £2,000 back within thirty days, how would that affect your thinking?

We need to manage our attraction and lead generation profitably. You can use a multitude of platforms to do this, but I recommend Facebook for most niches because it has the most comprehensive ad platform and the most powerful targeting features. Based on five years of using it to obtain a high return on ad spend, I developed the SIMPLE Method. You can use this method to start your own ad campaigns.

The SIMPLE Method

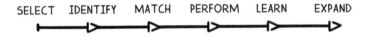

Figure 5.1 The SIMPLE Method

Step 1: Select. The first stage of any effective lead-generation campaign is to understand exactly who your target market is. One of the first exercises my clients complete on the Authority Accelerator is to define their customer avatar – a detailed profile of their ideal customer: their demographics, their interests and their pain points. The more defined your niche, the easier it is to find them.

Step 2: Identify. When you know who your target market is, you need to be able to find out where they are and how to communicate with them. All the ad platforms have targeting criteria that you can use to identify your niche. Facebook, along with Instagram (which shares the same ad platform), is a good all-rounder and is easiest to use. Some niches may be better suited to other platforms, such as LinkedIn, Google or YouTube.

The targeting criteria that are available are based on people's interests and behaviours on a specific platform. If only we could ask Facebook to create us an audience that contained only our perfect client type, life would be much simpler, but this is not the case. Therefore, depending on your niche, you may need to think in more depth about how to identify them. One effective method of finding your perfect client is to create an audience of people who have demonstrated an interest in your largest competitors. (If you already have a large presence on Facebook, to have people do this to you is the highest form of flattery!)

Step 3: Match. Now you've defined the audience you're going to market to, you need to build the ad itself. The key is to match a compelling message to the right market. To make sure your message stands out from the crowd immediately, you need a great hook. Most ads are made up of an image or a video, a headline and the body copy with a call to action. Always keep it as informal and organic as possible: this is social media after all, and the more something looks like an ad, the less people will be interested in it.

Use an organic image – ideally, something that places you in an authoritative environment and conveys your values – with a headline that conveys an outcome. That will capture your audience's attention. The body copy is more subjective, and I've seen effective copy in long-form and short-form adverts. Weave in elements of authority in the ad: this is someone's first contact point with you, so you need to make a good impression.

Step 4: Perform. Now you're ready to launch your ad – but how much should you spend? The algorithms behind the ad platforms are highly complex, evolving and delicate creatures, and we have to treat them with respect. They also 'self-learn' over the first few days of running, so they need to gather as much data as possible to optimise your ad placement for you. When you launch a new ad, therefore, you need to start with a small daily budget. This dramatically reduces your risk and exposure, while giving the algorithm time to learn and refine who it shows the ad to.

This is where many people go wrong. If you start a campaign with a large ad budget over a short space of time, the algorithm doesn't know what to do with the money you've given it, so it goes to the wrong places. A few years ago, someone told me that he'd 'given Facebook ads a go' to fill up a webinar he was hosting. He put in £1,000 but received just two signups. Essentially, he had forced far too much money into a small pipe, which caused the pipe to burst and spray his hard-earned cash all over the place.

Step 5: Learn. Within the bounds of the targeting you've set up, the algorithm will be learning who to show your ad to. Meanwhile, you can get quick feedback on the effectiveness of your ad and then optimise your ad using variations of audience and the creative elements. It's best not to touch your ad for the first three days of launching it, because it needs some time to settle. After three days, you'll see one of these results:

1. It's worked brilliantly first time

2. It's totally flopped

3. It's somewhere in the middle, and you can improve it through testing

The first two results are fairly unlikely: most of the time, you'll get some results that you can improve on. When testing to make changes, I always do so in the following order: audience, image, headline, copy. I rarely test variations on body copy, because optimising the audience and image usually brings an ad campaign within the parameters needed to be effective.

Step 6: Expand. When you're happy with your cost per lead, it's time to scale your ads. On an ad platform like Facebook, you'll probably run out of 'audience' to advertise to, because everyone in the interest-based audience you've built will have seen your ad. When this happens, you need to find some new audiences. You can start from scratch by using different targeting criteria, or you can create a 'lookalike' audience from the people you've already attracted.

This simple strategy, that can take just one click, gives you the most highly refined and targeted audience you can create at scale. Put simply, Facebook will look at the people you've attracted already, identify what they have in common and then build a new audience of the top 1% (or more, if you choose) of a country's population that matches them most closely. I've been working with lookalike audiences for years, and they consistently produce the best results for me and my clients in terms of return on ad spend.

Ultimately, lead generation is the lifeblood of your business. Whether you're attracting people to download a report, sign up to a webinar or watch a video on Facebook, without the systems in place for consistent and predictable lead generation you'll always have to hustle. Effective and profitable lead generation is a critical component to scaling your profits.

Ascension

You've now attracted and built an audience. By definition, your audience has demonstrated that they are relevant and engaged with your message, and that they are potential customers. Now you need to ascend your audience through your value chain so that they become loyal, high-paying clients.

People will *not* just click on your ad or watch your video and immediately buy your high-ticket services. You need to build an ascension process that accelerates the 'know, like, trust' process, raises your intrinsic value and puts the right offer in front of the right person at the right time.

After they've started to build an audience, many expert entrepreneurs do one of these things:

1. **Continue to nurture the audience by providing more and more value.** They then get stuck in the mindset that they can't put out offers in case they break the rapport and goodwill they've built up. This is the equivalent of the 'friend zone'.

2. **Only put out offers that don't nurture the audience or add value.** The audience goes for long periods without hearing from the expert and is then blasted with offers for a short time. This leads the audience to unsubscribe.

3. **Do nothing at all.** The audiences that the expert has created are rotting away, wasting all the time and money spent on building them. This is the most common scenario. Many people have a go at building a funnel, get some leads in, try to sell them something and then, when those leads don't buy immediately, they give up. The leads never hear from the expert again.

To avoid these scenarios, you need to build an ascension system that concurrently nurtures and presents ascension opportunities. By doing so, you will continue to develop the relationship with your audience, dramatically increase your customers' lifetime value and expose them to your offers regularly. It's important to put out ascension offers in a way that retains your audience's goodwill, so they don't feel you're switching from 'value mode' to 'sales mode'.

Nobody has the time to manually follow up all their leads, so you need to build a system that automates the bulk of the work. That frees you up to create new and engaging content and offers. But often, misconceptions get in the way of building these foundations:

1. **Lack of time.** This misconception stops you taking action to break the cycle. If you don't have enough time now, that proves that you need to build systems to offload some of the workload. To break the cycle, you need an intervention: either finding a mentor who will make you do it or blocking out a short period to focus on building the foundations.

2. **Overwhelm.** There are countless automation platforms on the market, with many people trying to sell you the latest funnel or hack that will bring in clients. The secret is that they all do almost the same thing! The tools might change regularly, but the fundamentals of human behaviour do not – so your focus should always be on the message, not the medium. If you feel overwhelmed, just pick a platform and see if it works for you and your niche.

3. **Cost.** Many people see the price of systems as an 'empty' cost rather than an investment – much like the situation with ad spend. Instead, look at this in terms of a time to effort ratio: how much your time is worth and how much time a platform saves you. If you're making £100,000

of sales a year then your hourly rate is about £50 an hour (assuming you're working a forty-hour week and taking a couple of weeks' holiday). If your systems can save you even a few hours of work a month, you'll be getting a return on your investment. And if you're selling anything with a decent premium, just one extra sale a year will cover your automation costs.

The power of follow-up

As a species, we need to be prompted to take action. Often, we need to hear the same message, or see the same offer, multiple times before it registers in our brains strongly enough for us to do something with it. We are constantly distracted and we often like to postpone taking action, thinking that we'll get round to it when it becomes more urgent.

It's important to understand this human trait, especially when we look at people's buying habits. As someone who invests a lot every year in personal development, and regularly joins high-level groups and masterminds, I do the same thing. We want the result, but we don't want to take the action that will get us there: getting our credit card out and paying for it!

As experts, this means we need to present our offer multiple times – and, if possible, in multiple mediums. In other words, we need to follow up.

The power of follow-up hit home when I ran that first webinar in the winter of 2015. Even though I made almost £5,000 of sales from that training, less than half of those sales were made during the event itself. The other half was generated by a simple three-part follow-up sequence that was sent by email through Infusionsoft to everyone who had attended the webinar but didn't buy.

Imagine how many sales you've left on the table by not following up with people: people who are your perfect client and need what you're offering, but who got distracted from taking the action they needed to.

CASE STUDY – RE-ENGAGING AUDIENCES BY FOLLOWING UP

When I started working with Mark, he was an established trainer in his marketplace, helping recruitment consultants scale. His credentials, record and branding were exemplary, and he had a sizeable database of email addresses, but he had reached capacity and needed help to scale up his business.

I identified three areas where Mark could get some immediate wins that would have a long-term impact on his market.

1. **Mark was trying to serve all levels of his target market.** That meant that he wasn't

communicating a focal message to a specific sub-niche. This had led to a multi-layered delivery model, and Mark was having to spread himself thin to deliver.

2. **Mark was predominantly working with clients on a one-to-one basis.** This was limiting the number of clients he could work with and capping his income. When added to the first point, this was creating a time and resourcing issue that limited Mark's growth and income.

3. **Because Mark was short of time, he was not able to nurture his existing audience.** He had fallen into the trap of creating an audience but then losing contact with it. He was not nurturing the asset that should have been generating all his wealth.

The result was that Mark didn't have enough time to focus on increasing reach and leveraging his expertise; he had become trapped in a hamster wheel. Our initial goal was to regain Mark's freedom to spend time with family, while increasing his income to create security. Here's what we did:

1. **We simplified Mark's model.** We did this by picking the sub-niche that Mark felt he could serve most effectively. We also made his delivery models leaner, and decided to focus on one core offer, followed by an ongoing support programme that could be delivered to an unlimited amount of clients at once and

delivered Mark a recurring monthly revenue stream; he didn't have to 'resell' it every month.

2. **We replaced the one-to-one programme with a group coaching programme.** We then re-framed Mark's offer to communicate the outcome that he was providing for his clients. We also shortened the length of the programme from six months to three months. People want to achieve a result as quickly as possible but given a longer period of time to do it, they will use all of that time. In Mark's case, the work that was being done in six months could actually be done in three. In addition, you can charge the same for a group coaching programme as you can for a one-to-one programme, while getting better results from the group dynamic.

3. **We created a re-engagement and follow-up campaign for Mark's existing audiences.** After he sold the first two programme places to his organic network, we put the entire database into the follow-up sequence.

Two weeks later, Mark had sold another four places. He had gained almost £10,000 of sales by re-framing his offer and communicating it effectively to his existing audience. Even more impressively, he achieved all of this with no course name, marketing materials or even a programme start date. There was just an outcome, and Mark was able to communicate that to his audience.

Summary

When you use the Triple A Method effectively, you will rapidly and dramatically increase your lead flow and conversions. That means it's important that you can handle higher numbers of client. If you're providing one-to-one support, trading time for money, you'll hit that glass ceiling and more leads will create huge operational issues and stress. To overcome this, you need to ensure that your delivery models are optimised and designed for scale while maintaining high profit margins. The next chapter moves on to this aspect of the method.

CHAPTER FIVE: EXERCISES

Check through this automation tools checklist to help prepare:

1. **CRM.** You will need to select a customer relationship management system, to store and manage all of the contact records in your database. Many modern CRMs come as part of an autoresponder.

2. **Autoresponder.** An autoresponder gives you the ability to automate the follow up with email leads, putting them in sequences which deliver calls to action at the right place and right time. Some of the better-known autoresponders and CRMs include Clickfunnels, Active Campaign and Infusionsoft. I use Infusionsoft.

3. **Facebook business page.** To run lead generation through Facebook, you will need a Facebook Business page. There are several types of 'business' page you can set, I recommend you create a public figure page which will communicate you and your values while building rapport with your audience more effectively.

4. **Facebook ad account.** The second requirement to run Facebook ads is the ad account itself, which is used to create the ads, run them and pay for them.

5. **Diary booking system.** When you're generating lead flow, you need the ability for those leads to book into your diary without you having to manually arrange it. There are several platforms that are simple to use and will integrate into your auto-responder system. I recommend Acuity or Calendly.

CHAPTER SIX

Amplify

M any expert entrepreneurs want to create a business where they can generate income streams with a high profit margin that are built around their lifestyle. Be it to travel, to spend time with family, or even to generate cash flow while creating longer-term wealth through other business activities, the concept of building freedom and choice should lie at the heart of your business model.

All too often, I speak to experts who have created delivery models that mean they can never take a break without losing all their momentum and significant income in the process. This chapter looks at the cross section of delivery models that you can build your ecosystem around and outlines the simplest route to achieving mobility alongside high profit margins.

The Freedom Formula

I created the Freedom Formula to demonstrate where various delivery models sit on the 'profit-to-effort ratio' curve. This is a graph plotting the profit-to-effort ratio against different programme types to show what delivery mechanism gives highest profit for minimum effort, which therefore leads to financial freedom.

The profit-to-effort ratio is an indicator of how much profit you'll make with your delivery model compared with the amount of work you put in to market, sell and provide it. It is not a measure of absolute profit. For example, if you make £1,000 of profit every time you make a sale, but you have to work 100 hours to deliver it, your ratio of profit-to-effort will be low. Conversely, if you make £100 of profit every time you make a sale, but it only takes you ten minutes to deliver it, your ratio of profit-to-effort will be much higher, even though your total profit is lower.

As we move up the price point scale, the profit-to-effort ratio creates an inverted bell curve, which we can split into three sections.

Section 1 contains the lowest price point delivery models. They include continuity programmes, membership websites and digital programmes. Models in this section have a low price point and a high volume. If you

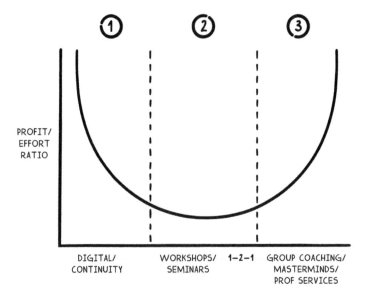

Figure 6.1 The Freedom Formula – profit-to-effort curve

get this model right, you can achieve a lot of leverage: it takes no more time to sell and deliver a thousand products than it does to sell and deliver one.

The main drawback with pure digital products is that they don't achieve great results for your clients. This is because they focus more on providing information, and less on implementation and accountability. That makes the product more difficult to sell: people are looking for implementation rather than information, and they are jaded by buying digital programmes and never doing anything with them.

Section 2 contains the models that, in general, will give you the worst return for your effort. These include one-to-one coaching and workshops. Some people may be able to charge upwards of £20,000 for a twelve-month one-to-one package or fill a workshop with seventy people paying £1,000 each, but these are the exceptions to the norm. More often, people charge an hourly rate (£20 to £40 an hour) for one-to-one services and charge less than £200 a day for a workshop. When you charge for yourself at an hourly rate, you're immediately devaluing your worth and building a thick glass ceiling for your income.

Many people attempt to make the jump from one-to-one delivery to workshop delivery, but this model also has inherent flaws when building profit margins at scale. Your market will see geographical and time issues as barriers. When you factor in the other expenses involved – venue hire, lunch, refreshments, audio-visual systems and events staff – and the risk of not filling the workshop (and so de-positioning yourself in front of your audience), you rapidly start wondering whether the outcome is worth the effort.

Section 3 contains models that are at a premium price point. As such, they are generally sold in lower volumes. These models include group coaching, mastermind groups and some professional services. Professional service models are outside the scope of this book, but the strategies to attract 'done for you' clients are the same as the ones you will use for 'done-with-you' programmes. If you are running a professional services model, however, it must be high margin and either require low regular input from you (such as a Facebook ads service) or be possible to delegate it to a team (eg a content marketing service). Don't get tied into a lower-profit-margin, high-input professional service model that you can't scale.

What constitutes high ticket is subjective and will vary from niche to niche. In general, the lower end of high-ticket pricing starts at £1,000, the middle is in the £2,500 to £10,000 bracket, and anything over £10,000 is at the high end. You may even have an 'Uber' high-ticket offering that is significantly more expensive (think £50,000 or more) that is rarely used.

High-ticket models are still leverageable, but not infinitely so. They are the quickest route to scaling to a six-figure profit margin without having to completely redesign your business models.

There is no right or wrong model for you to use, and programme design is not an exact science. Look to take the elements that work best for your niche and scale them. Just because something works well for me, or one of my clients, doesn't mean it will work well for you. Often, the most effective programmes are hybrids that take the best parts of multiple models and mix them up a little.

Remember, all good programmes need to offer a tangible outcome that your market can visualise. This is why I favour models that are entirely focused on implementation, rather than those that just teach information and leave your market to work out what to do with it themselves. Here are my preferred models for creating those results and the average price points for each one.

Model 1: The membership website

Depending on your niche, you can charge from £10 to £100 a month for access to a membership website. The components of an effective membership website are:

- **An on-demand library of digital programmes**, which users can consume when required. Think Netflix, but for your niche.

- **A forum**, where you create community within the membership site. This helps your students to implement the training and when you get to a certain scale the forum will become self-sustaining: you will no longer need to prompt engagement. People love to be part of a tribe, and by having an engaged group that is genuinely benefiting from membership, you will reduce the rate at which members leave and you have to bring on new ones.

- **Led sessions** that provide some form of coaching and accountability, whether you or your team deliver them. When you're getting started, it is best to lead them yourself, because you're the reason the members are there in the first place. Sessions could be weekly, fortnightly or monthly, depending on the niche and price point.

If you charged a membership fee of £50 a month, 100 members would give you £5,000 a month, and 200 members would give you £10,000 a month. Following this through, if you have the systems in place to attract 200 members, with an effective marketing and re-investment strategy you can scale this to 2,000 members and be hitting over seven figures in annual revenue.

You will have a member churn rate: the rate at which members leave and you have to find new ones. From my experience across multiple businesses and working with multiple clients, this is around 25%. If your target is to reach, say, 200 members in the group, you'll need to be on-boarding fifty new members every month as fifty others leave. Another issue with a membership website is that it is more difficult to sell a subscription than it is to sell a one-off product. We have a habit of regarding subscriptions as endless, and providers often fail to convey the outcome effectively, so it's even more important to pitch it to the right person at the right time.

Model 2: The 'accelerator' group coaching structure

Group coaching gives you the best blend of leveraging your expertise, scaling the model, creating a flexible delivery structure and making high-margin profits. I always structure my group coaching programmes as a ninety-day 'accelerator' style event, and my clients have had success with this too.

As well as fitting neatly into the quarterly goal-setting cycle, ninety days is the perfect length of time to follow a process from A to B and see results for your clients. It's natural to feel that the longer the programme is, the higher its perceived value will be – but this is simply not true. To structure a programme like that means you are trying to pad the value out, rather than sell the outcome.

The elements of an effective group programme are:

- **It must be outcome-driven and follow the A to B roadmap.** By the end of ninety days, the client should have achieved the aim of the programme with tangible results that can be measured.

- **Some content should be digitised.** Don't waste valuable coaching time by teaching the same information over and over again – digitise the content itself so your client can access it when they want and consume it at their own pace.

- **It must include group coaching calls.** Hold a group coaching call every week for the ninety days (this equates to thirteen sessions). Schedule them at the same time every week to get into an effective routine – results are important!

- **It must have a support forum.** You'll need a support forum between sessions so your clients can get their questions answered and you can provide accountability updates. This could be a Facebook or WhatsApp group, but Slack is a more professional platform for service delivery.

Group coaching programmes usually start at £1,500 for a place and cost up to £5,000 at the higher end. Assuming a price point of £2,500, and the ability to put ten people in a group, you will be achieving £25,000 of sales per course. While you're getting started, rather than overlapping intakes you can run four 90-day programme starts every year, taking you to the six-figure turnover bracket with a mere forty clients.

When your group has finished the ninety days and achieved the outcome, their focus is likely to shift to the next level, which presents the opportunity to offer them a follow-on programme.

Model 3: Continuity

In any A to B outcome-based programme, arriving at point B is rarely the ultimate goal. As expert entrepreneurs, one of our biggest drivers is growth, so the chances of you wanting to stand still are close to zero.

For example, on the Authority Accelerator I work with my clients to build out the four phases of growing a high-ticket expert business. Phase 1 is defining your market, message and models. Phase 2 is positioning you and accelerating your authority to rapidly raise your intrinsic value. Phase 3 is building out the full value ecosystem, and Phase 4 is attracting traffic into it. During the ninety days, we do real-world exercises to drive organic traffic and make 'low-hanging fruit' sales to test the concepts and gain momentum. We build all the foundations so my clients can leverage them over the next year or so.

The work with those clients doesn't finish after ninety days. After we've built the programme, we need to gather the data, optimise and scale the campaigns to keep growing profitably. At this point, I hand over to my Inner Circle, which is a continuity programme for growth. A continuity programme should provide support and accountability as well as introducing more advanced concepts and techniques.

What you can charge for a continuity programme varies considerably by niche and input, but it will range from

£100 to £1000 a month. Let's take the figures discussed in the group coaching illustration and assume that you introduce a continuity programme priced at £500 a month. You achieve a 20% conversion rate (which is conservative) from the forty clients who went through your accelerator. You now have eight clients paying you a combined recurring revenue of £4,000 a month. This is on top of the initial sales, and without having to spend time, energy or advertising budget on acquiring a new customer.

CASE STUDY – GROWTH THROUGH CONTINUITY

When Brett joined my Authority Accelerator programme, he had a wealth of experience in a small niche of the property development industry. Brett was concerned about whether his niche was too narrow, and he didn't want to saturate it.

I always help clients develop their product ecosystem around their personal goals, because one size doesn't fit all. We created a programme that gave Brett a huge profit margin compared to the effort he needed to run it, with a high-value, low-volume monthly group mentorship model.

As with any programme, we engineered it to accelerate Brett's clients' results, offer implementation support, and increase the lifetime customer value. It was a partnership model that would lead to the highest ticket returns in the medium term.

Brett tested the new offer by presenting it to existing audiences, as this does not involve any extra acquisition costs. As a result, six people enrolled on Brett's beta programme, each paying £500 a month. Brett was now receiving payments of £3,000 a month, just by creating a few social media posts and making some phone calls. This led to a partnership with another property trainer, which brought in a five-figure sum for a one-day workshop. At this stage, Brett realised that his pricing wasn't quite right and doubled it to £1,000 a month.

We then started to build out Brett's client acquisition ecosystem, but in all honesty, clients kept on coming to him organically. Brett now has £7,000 a month of recurring revenue without using the paid-for client acquisition systems.

The next step is to scale this with paid-for attraction methods: first, to get past the five-figure monthly milestone, and then to ensure the models are optimised for revenue of £30,000 a month in the next six to twelve months.

Why you should start high ticket

There is no right or wrong delivery model, and designing your model isn't an exact science. Always focus on creating a model that works for you and your niche.

The price point of your programme will add to or detract from your authority-building process. Generally, the higher the price of your services, the more authority will be associated with them. We live in a world dominated by brands; often, merely adding a big brand logo to an item of clothing more than doubles what someone will pay for it. We have been conditioned, culturally, to associate price with quality, and so it follows that higher price points themselves create the perception of intrinsic value and a higher-quality programme.

You still need to show that other people are willing to pay that price point. If you have no social proof, you can't pick a high figure out of the air and hope people will pay it. Instead, you have to incrementally increase your price point at the same time as raising your authority. I call this the 'authority loop' (see Figure 6.2). It is a method of compounding your authority and raising your value through continual results.

As well as creating authority alchemy, operating a premium model benefits your business by allowing you to spend much more to acquire a customer. To illustrate this point, we're going to have to do a bit of maths.

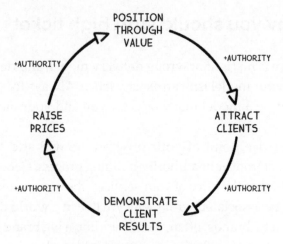

Figure 6.2 The authority loop

Maximum acquisition cost (MAC)

One metric you should be setting in your business is how much you're prepared to pay to acquire a customer. This is your MAC. A good rule of thumb is to use a MAC of 50% of your profit before ad spend.

To illustrate, let's assume that your premium product has no direct sales or delivery costs other than the ad spend, and you set the sale price at £2,000. Using a MAC of 50% means you are happy to pay £1,000 in ad costs to make the sale – giving you a return of 2:1 on your ad spend. (Remember, this is the **maximum** acquisition cost that you would be prepared to pay. When you build an effective value ecosystem, you will see much higher returns on your ad spend: 5:1 or 10:1 is fairly common.)

If you're selling a low-ticket item – say, a digital product for £100 – then by using a MAC of 50% you can now only spend £50 to acquire that customer and still make your margins. Because your lead generation is independent of your sales, your cost per lead will usually be the same in both instances. In other words, whether you're generating leads for a webinar that's selling a £100 product or a £2,000 product, there will be no difference in your cost per lead onto the webinar.

To illustrate the point and keep the maths simple, let's say it costs you £5 a lead to get someone to sign up for this webinar. To hit your targets with the low-ticket product, you will have to make at least one sale from every ten leads generated (10 leads at £5 a lead is £50 of ad spend to make one £100 sale). You need to achieve a 10% conversion rate to hit your targets.

To hit your targets with the high-ticket product, you only need to make one sale from every 200 leads generated (200 leads at £5 a lead is £1,000 of ad spend to make one £2,000 sale). With the high-ticket model, you only need to achieve a 0.5% conversion rate to maintain your MAC, which is much easier and less risky to achieve. That means you would need to make twenty sales of the low-ticket product to make the same amount of profit as you would for selling just one of your high-ticket programmes.

At this point, you might be asking, 'But surely my conversion rates will be much higher when selling the £100 programme than when selling the £2,000 programme?' The conversion rates may be slightly higher, but nowhere near high enough to make the equation comparable for both cases. I've seen many instances where a programme with a low price point actually gets *worse* conversion rates than the one with a high price. That's directly attributable to the outcome of the programme, in that the higher priced programme has an end goal, whereas the low-price programme is more general, which we've been discussing in such depth.

Momentum

Momentum is your final advantage when starting with high-ticket services. We now need to look at the total amount of money you're bringing in, rather than percentages.

The example calculations in the previous section showed that to make the same net profit, the conversion rate you need is much lower for a high-ticket product than for a low-ticket product. Therefore, you don't need to have as large an audience in place to make the same profit with a high-ticket product.

If you start with a high-ticket product, you will have larger chunks of income arriving in your bank account when you make sales. This gives you options and momentum. You can re-invest your profits into expanding your audiences, creating more trust, generating more leads and compounding your sales. You could hire an outsourced team to take over the web design and building, copywriting and running your ads, freeing you up to spend time building your authority.

When you've been growing your audiences through a high-ticket offer, there will come a point where it's time to introduce the lower ticket offer to increase the overall sales per lead in your ecosystem. This is simply done by taking the content you've been teaching and turning it into a digital product which you can then sell at a much higher volume, albeit with a lower price point.

Summary

The Triple A Method is a simple framework. First, you need to build awareness by bridging your market's pain/problem gap, leading them to the point of illumination and transferring their attention to your unique and de-commoditised process. Concurrently, you need to build your authority and intrinsic value, so your market trusts you enough to use your services at a price point that reflects the true value you deliver. Finally, you need to ensure the process is automated so you can increase your reach, leverage your expertise and push through the glass ceiling that's currently preventing you from having full control over your lifestyle.

Although the Triple A Method is straightforward, the process of following it is not easy. You need a system for using the method in the real world, making the most of the tools you have access to right now. Next, we'll look at how you can build out your own value ecosystem to put the Triple A Method into practice.

CHAPTER SIX: EXERCISES

To help generate income streams with a high profit margin that are built around their lifestyle, consider the following steps and questions.

1. Select your delivery model from the freedom formula. My recommendation is to start with a high price point, low volume model in Section 3 to get momentum in your business.

2. What is the outcome for the client? Define the ultimate outcome of someone enrolling on your programme; for example, the outcome of the Authority Accelerator is to build a system that is attracting high value leads that are converting onto your high-ticket programmes within 90 days.

3. What are the stepping stones your client must take to achieve the outcome? Again, to use the

example of the Authority Accelerator, we go through four stages:

   i. Crafting your power message and structuring your delivery models

  ii. Accelerating your authority

 iii. Building your ecosystem

 iv. Attracting relevant leads

4. What price point is your delivery model? When you set your price point, always think about what return your client will get on the programme, not how much it costs you to deliver it in time and money.

CHAPTER SEVEN

Your Power Message

How do you find the time and resources to position yourself as the go-to authority, at scale, when the platforms you are using are already saturated with competition, have a declining organic reach and are increasing their ad costs? How can you make an inefficient system effective again?

The answer lies in thinking differently. Rather than trying to out-shout, out-hustle and outspend your competitors, you need to change the paradigm and do less. Less noise, less ad spend and smaller audiences.

But much more highly targeted.

If you can identify the subsection of your market that is the most relevant and engaged with your message early, you can focus all your resources on developing a deep relationship with a much smaller audience. You will then be able to dominate their attention with ease.

The value ecosystem

Think about the funnel that's been used since the dawn of marketing time.

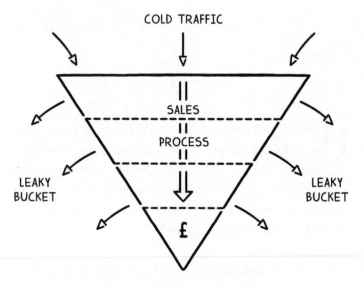

Figure 7.1 Traditional sales funnel

With the right systems in place, this can work – but it's extremely inefficient. You spend all your money and effort on putting unqualified leads in at the top, most of which fall out of the numerous holes on the way to the bottom, where you hope to make a sale that will give you a return on your investment.

The other flaw with this model is that a funnel is designed to progress cold leads to a sale, rather than to develop a relationship with them. How can you build those relationships when the vast majority of leads fall out and disappear? To sell premium services (which nearly all expert products and services are), you need to build that strong relationship first.

To transform the old-school funnel into a relevant sales and marketing system, all you need to do is turn the funnel upside down. Rather than filling the large end of the funnel with unqualified leads, you're going to fill the tiny end with highly engaged and targeted audiences. Rather than being squeezed and falling out of the holes, your leads can spread out into the larger part of the funnel, where they will now stay in an open loop of value. In other words, now you've captured them, you can control the content and messaging that gets distributed to them. Using a strategic messaging structure, you can keep developing that relationship consistently over time until your leads feel compelled to reach out to you and ascend themselves to the next level.

This is the value ecosystem, and it's got some major benefits for you, the expert entrepreneur:

1. **It's easy to set up.** To make this work, all you need to do is identify those who have engaged with you to create your initial audience, and then identify the tools to put them in the open loop

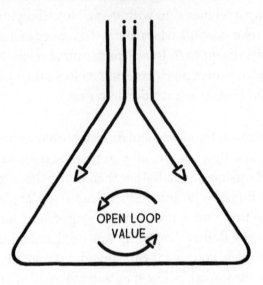

ENGAGED + RELEVANT TRAFFIC

OPEN LOOP VALUE

Figure 7.2 Value ecosystem

value. Social media platforms make it possible to do this without having any technical ability at all. You can set up your value ecosystem with nothing more than a smartphone and a Facebook account.

2. **It's automated.** After you've set up your ecosystem, you can focus on creating valuable content. The system will look after the distribution for you, meaning you can concentrate on being in the zone of genius and flow.

3. **It's cheap.** Because you're only building a relationship with people who have already

engaged with you (through your organic or paid-for marketing activities), you'll be nurturing a small audience. It costs very little to achieve consistency in front of that audience, giving the impression that you're everywhere. This aids the authority-building process.

There are five elements of the value ecosystem:

1. The power message

2. Attractors

3. Magnetisers

4. Primers

5. Calls to action

The rest of this chapter focuses on how to craft your power message.

Rocket fuel for your business

Before you build your ecosystem, you must first craft the message that will power it. Think of your ecosystem as a Formula One car engine, highly tuned and powerful, with the ability to take you to places quicker than any other car. To make that engine work at its full potential, you need to put the right fuel in. Your power message is the high-octane fuel that goes into your engine and makes it run. It's the foundation of everything you will do.

Most of the ads I see on Facebook claim to reveal the latest secret, hack, software or platform that you can use to generate more clients and sales. But none of this matter if you don't have a messaging system that brings your market to the realisation that they can achieve the outcome you're offering and that they want you to help them achieve it. The platforms and tactics are just the delivery mechanisms for your message, and the reality is that most expert entrepreneurs are not delivering the right message. This is why it's vital to get your power message right before you think about how you will deliver it.

It's even possible that you're delivering a message that is de-positioning you in front of your audience. This happens when there's a fundamental mismatch between your market and your message. The mismatch creates a conflict, which usually manifests as negativity towards your content and adverts, dismantling any authority you've built up. Luckily, there is a system you can use to avoid that mismatch.

Your 'one thing'

Before you can craft your power message, it's fundamental to understand what you do and for whom. It never ceases to surprise me when I ask people what they do and they don't have an immediate answer. If you're not sure what you do, how will your market ever know? We need to find your magic power: the one thing you can do better than anyone else and that you want to be known as an authority for.

There are two steps to this: what you do, and who you do it for.

What do you do?

This is the value you bring to the world. Focus on something that you're *actually* amazing at; faking it until you make it is not a recommended strategy for becoming an expert. Ask yourself these questions:

- What value do I bring to the world?
- What am I emotionally connected to?
- What is my identity?

To truly establish yourself as the authority in your niche, you need to answer all three questions. If any of them are unanswered, you will probably lack the drive to build your business properly. Here is an example from my own experience.

CASE STUDY: WORKING IN FLOW

When I launched PEG, the property industry seemed to be the logical niche in which to start my first training business. I had achieved success in the property world myself, and I wanted to set up a business that would create cash flow (property is a cash-intensive industry) while helping others push through a barrier that I could see them hitting. PEG grew quickly, but after eighteen months something odd happened: although the financial metrics were looking fantastic, I started to dread showing up. Showing up with content, showing up at events, showing up for our clients. I lost the motivation and was experiencing an inner conflict.

When I sat down and chatted this through, I came to the realisation that I wasn't emotionally connected to the medium itself – property. This is, of course, an issue when you're running a property training company. I came to the conclusion that I was emotionally connected to the process of training rather than to property, which I saw as an objective wealth-generation mechanism rather than a passion I wanted to be immersed in. My intrinsic drive to make a difference was much stronger.

I also realised there was a disconnect with my identity. I had always thought of myself as a 'property guy', whereas the reality was that I was a trainer. Although I could bring value to the property niche through my experience, I was not emotionally connected to it and it was in conflict with my true identity. That put up a huge barrier to growth.

The result was that I pivoted to helping other expert entrepreneurs build impactful and scalable businesses that reached more people and created a lifestyle built around freedom.

This is not as 'fluffy' as it might sound. Understanding your true identity and what you're connected to is a key to high performance that will unlock your innate potential. Becoming self-aware can take years of reflection and experience, but you can make a start by taking some time to reflect on your inherent motivators and drivers.

Once you have answered the three questions, you need to focus on what you do for your market. This is your magic power, so it has to be specific. In an attempt to cater for a wider market, many experts make the mistake of being too broad and generic about what they do. Don't fall into this trap: speak and appeal to as small a market as you can, so you can communicate in their language and narrowly focus your resources to find them.

Here are some examples of how you can narrow down broader niches into magic powers that say precisely what you do:

Niche	Sub-niche (magic power)
Business coaching	Client acquisition
	Strategy
	Business plan creation
	Fundraising
	Partnerships
	Branding
	Team-building
	Systemisation
Health and fitness coaching	Nutrition-based weight loss
	Keto diet
	Fasting
	High-intensity interval training
Marketing agency	Content marketing
	Facebook pay-per-click
	Google
	LinkedIn
	Web development
	Search engine optimisation (SEO)
	Copywriting

Who do you do it for?

After you've decided on your magic power, you need to think about the precise demographic you're serving. To use the Triple A Method, you need to bridge the pain/problem gap. Different markets have different problems, so you need to be able to communicate the real problem that a specific market feels. When you choose your niche market, you need to think about both the demographic or industry *and* the stage that they are at.

Let's say your magic power is client acquisition. Although all service businesses are looking for more clients, you need to start by choosing an industry to focus on. You decide to concentrate on physiotherapists – so your niche is now 'helping physiotherapists to attract more clients'. However, you can break down the physiotherapist niche further by looking at what stage of business growth they are in. Are they in the start-up phase, in early stage growth or scaling and looking to open multiple branches?

This is important because the pain/problem gap will be different depending on the stage of growth your client is at. In addition, to gain awareness and attract attention, you need to speak their language and create a message that resonates. There would be little point in projecting a message about how to create and scale a centralised marketing strategy for multi-branch physiotherapists and putting it in front of start-up solopreneurs who are bootstrapping their way to their first few clients.

This same principle applies regardless of whether your niche is business or consumer. For example, if you're a fitness coach, you could niche down to weight loss after having a baby, which has a different set of pains and problems from the niche of nutrition for high-performance athletes.

Your core messaging structure

Your niche is stuck in pain for a reason: they have a problem that they have not been able to fix so far. Either they don't know what their problem is yet, which is why we must build awareness, or they simply don't believe they can make the change and get the results that you're offering. Almost everyone has some form of limiting belief system that holds them back, and this creates barriers and objections:

- 'It won't work in my niche'

- 'I don't have the technical ability'

- 'I've got no money to invest in this'

- 'I haven't got the time'

- 'I don't want to take the risk'

Self-limiting beliefs all boil down to some form of fear. Our fears can be split into five main categories: extinction, mutilation, loss of autonomy, separation and ego-death.[1] All the fears we experience can be associated with one or more of these categories. For example, you may have a limiting belief about paid-for advertising. You may fear that you'll lose all your cash by investing in ads, which means you can't use it for things you want to spend it on: this is a fear of loss of autonomy. Alternatively, you may fear that when you start advertising, people will 'find out that you are a fraud' and reject you: fear of separation. Or you may fear that you'll start attracting negativity, criticism and trolls: fear of ego death.

Over ten years of coaching, I have found that limiting beliefs are formed through experience and are then internalised, but they are almost certainly false. To help bring your audience to the point of illumination, we must create a framework that helps them to overcome these barriers.

The core pillars of messaging

The first stage is to create an overarching theme for your content and message: a theme that reflects how you do things differently from everyone else. This is

---

1 K. Albrecht, 'The (Only) 5 Fears We All Share' (*Psychology Today*, 2012), www.psychologytoday.com/gb/blog/brainsnacks/201203/the-only -5-fears-we-all-share

the classic 'old world versus new world' or 'us versus them' narrative, which is powerful in attracting an audience based on a contrast you create.

Look at the theme running though this section. If we use the 'old world versus new world' storyline then funnel marketing is the old and ineffective way of marketing, and the value ecosystem is the new way. This works for the 'us versus them' storyline as well. In this case, 'them' would be marketers who use tactics based on scarcity and urgency to sell their goods or services, while 'us' is the expert entrepreneur who is looking to create awareness, build an audience and provide value before looking for the sale. Of course, your theme must be real and not something that has been made up to manipulate your market.

After you've derived your theme, the next step is to create the core messaging pillars that will prop it up. This is the message that will bring the content consumer to the point of realising that they can change their lives.

To do this, write down what you consider to be the three biggest objections your market has to achieving the results that you offer. Keep this big picture; the chances are that there will be plenty of sub-themes to address as well. If you're struggling to identify those three objections, go out to your market and ask. There are plenty of free resources at your disposal; for example, you could put out a poll in a Facebook group that your niche belongs to.

Overcoming these three objections will become your core pillars of messaging. The majority of the content that you make public should follow one of these themes. Over time, as your audience consumes more of your content, they will move from a point of fear to a point of belief, which then opens their minds to the reality that they can achieve their goals with your help.

I hope you can see how much more powerful this is than putting out content for the sake of publishing content. If the content you post is irrelevant, you may as well not post at all.

To illustrate this technique, here is my 'one thing' and my three core pillars of messaging:

One thing

I help expert entrepreneurs strategically scale their reach, impact and profit by exploding their authority.

Pillar 1: Premium pricing is good.

Many experts feel that they are either not worthy of charging a premium price and will get 'found out', or that their market will not pay a premium price. Because their motivation is to help people, they often have the (mistaken) belief that not charging high rates will attract more clients and help more people.

In reality, when you've followed the Triple A Method, premium pricing is easier to sell, brings you better quality clients and gives you momentum in your business. This momentum gives you the resources to reach and make a difference to more people, more quickly, and puts you in a state of flow that attracts more clients to you.

Pillar 2: You don't have to be a tech genius to leverage your expert business.

Most experts restrict their growth to organic and 'hustle' tactics because they believe that scaling requires complex and expensive technology and a large team to implement it. The reality is that technology has never been simpler for everyone to use. You no longer need to understand coding or need any design skills to build all the systems you need to move your business into the six-figure profit bracket; you can do it all with just a smartphone and Facebook account.

Pillar 3: Investing in ad spend is the least risky and easiest way to grow your business.

Many people believe that investing in ads is akin to taking your hard-earned profits and flushing them down the toilet. They believe that advertising is a black art that doesn't really work.

When you've structured your business correctly, the reality is that you can build significant momentum before you switch to paid-for ads. When you do have some profits in the bank, you can invest them in ads in a way that minimises risk. Because ads are simple to set up and give us real-time data, we can see quickly that for every £1 we put in, we'll get a specific amount out. As long as your ads are making a profit, you can then scale them, keeping an eye on that return. The moment the ads are not making a profit, you can turn them off or optimise them to make them profitable again.

Summary

In this chapter we've looked at the importance of crafting a power message to your market who knows exactly what you do, who you serve and what they need to believe to be true to work with you. When you create content based around your core pillars of messaging, you'll build up a library that you can re-use to put across a consistent message and rapidly bring your market to that point of belief. Without a core messaging strategy, regardless of the engagement you may get with your content, it will be fundamentally superficial, and it will not drive your audiences into your ascension systems.

In the next chapter we will look at how to build those systems.

CHAPTER SEVEN: EXERCISES

Consider the following questions and points to help distil your power message.

What is your magic power? What **exactly** do you do? Do you help with paid-for advertising, decreasing body fat, sourcing high yielding property investments in the North West, and so on?

1. What niche do you serve? What sub-set of an industry, eg professional services is too wide, you could narrow it down to marketing agencies, accountants, and so on. You can even take this a step further and sub-niche to pay-per-click marketing agencies, or family law offices, for example.

2. What stage is your niche at (eg if a business niche, is it start-up, early stage growth or scaling)?

3. Remember the core messaging Pillars 1, 2 and 3.

CHAPTER EIGHT

Building Your Value Ecosystem

Now you've created your messaging framework, you need to build out your ecosystem to attract the right people and ascend them to become paying clients. Your ecosystem will consist of attractors, magnetisers, primers and calls to action.

Attractors

Your attractors work in the same way that a light bulb attracts a moth. By putting your power message in front of your niche, you will naturally pull in those people who resonate with not only your message but also you and your values. This is why it was important to carry out the value matching exercise in Chapter Four. Once you have put out your message and attracted your perfect audience, you will need a mechanism for communicating with them further, so any attraction system must also be able to capture your audience so you can start to nurture those relationships.

Here are some tools you can use as attractors:

Attraction method 1: The lead magnet

The lead magnet is a value exchange: to receive something of value for free, the consumer must first provide their contact details. This is also known as 'gated content': there is a gate that someone must pass through to access it.

Ever since the invention of email marketing, the lead magnet has been used to capture people's email addresses. A database of email addresses should still be part of your ecosystem, regardless of changes in the expert industry and new ways of bringing in clients. By definition, an ecosystem has multiple layers, and an email database forms one of those layers.

Today, there are many ways in which you can carry out a value exchange and capture contact details other than an email address. In a world of declining email open and click-through rates, we need to look for other mediums through which to communicate. You can use the following mediums to capture contact details in exchange for value:

- **Facebook lead ads.** This is a simple and tech-free way of setting up a lead-generation campaign without having to build landing pages and autoresponders. You can use the Facebook Lead Ad to put an opt-in form on Facebook in no more than a couple of minutes. You can then download the contact details from Facebook or integrate them with an autoresponder if you have one.

- **Chatbots.** By delivering lead magnets through a chatbot on social media, you encourage consumers to opt in to a chatbot list. Subsequent communications will be through the platform's direct messenger, rather than by email. There has been a surge in uptake of chatbots recently, accompanied by a huge rise in open rates and, therefore, click-through rates. Most people have push notifications enabled on their phone, so it's hard to ignore that message when it pops up on their home screen.

Many people ask me what type of lead magnet they should create. Here are some rules of thumb:

1. It should be consumable in no more than twenty minutes

2. The consumer should be able to use the information immediately

3. It must be relevant to the service you are ultimately providing

4. It must build your authority and intrinsic value and take the consumer through the awareness process by highlighting the pain/problem gap and explaining your unique frameworks

Lead magnets can range from infographics to full-day discovery events. The more time and effort someone needs to invest to consume the lead magnet, the lower the conversion rate will be and the more expensive each lead will be. However, they will also be more relevant. If you're giving away a 'cheat sheet', your leads will be cheaper, but many will be 'junk leads'. If you're offering a free event, it may cost you more than £50 to get an opt-in, but that lead will be much more relevant.

For me, a healthy medium communicates your processes and delivers value for a price point that is scalable. In general, I recommend a report style lead magnet to my clients, but your optimum lead magnet will depend on your industry.

Attraction method 2: Self-hosted content

The issue with 'gated content' such as a lead magnet is that markets are increasingly sceptical about parting with their valuable contact information. Even if they do opt in with their details, an increasing number of email systems will then filter out your follow-up.

Essentially, your market knows that when they opt into something, they're going to receive some marketing communications.

To overcome this problem, you can use 'un-gated content' as an attractor. There is no opt-in process required for the consumer to access the content, so the 'salesperson barrier' is not triggered. However, you need to make sure that you can still follow up with the people who are consuming the content. The social media platforms have solved this problem neatly for us, as we can track the activity that happens on our website – including our lead magnet content – by placing a cookie (or a pixel, if you're using Facebook) on the pages you want to track. If this sounds complicated, you can outsource it for less than five pounds.

This means we can now host content on our websites and promote it through social media posts. Anyone who clicks through to consume the content will fall into your follow-up audience so you can start the process of nurturing them. If you want to refine this, you can segment your leads by the length of time that they spend on a particular page. For example, you might decide that you only want to capture the top 25% of people who have read your blog, based on the length of time they've spent on your page.

Attraction method 3: Native content

Attraction method 2 is powerful, but it still involves directing people away from the social media platform they were browsing, which will create a friction point in the process. (That said, anything that does create a friction point means that those who do click through will be highly relevant).

To remove that friction point and build rapid awareness in our markets, you can create engagement audiences from content you publish on the social media platforms themselves. This is called 'native content'. You can publish native content on many platforms, but I use Facebook and Instagram. On those platforms, you can use the following methods to create audiences through engagement with native content:

1. **Post engagement.** When you post content on a business page (this is important, because it won't work on your personal profile), anyone who engages with it will fall into your 'nurture' audiences. 'Engagement' includes likes, comments and shares of your content. Because Facebook and Instagram share the same ad platform, it will work on content you put on both, and it is simple to set up.

2. **Video views.** This is the game changer when it comes to building your reach and authority and bringing the best audiences into your value

ecosystem. Put simply, whenever you post a video as native content on Facebook, you can create a 'video view audience' and specify on a granular level who will go into it. You can specify who goes into an audience by choosing from the following view time options: anyone who has watched 3 seconds, 10 seconds, 25%, 50%, 75% or 100% of your video. Your core messaging videos should be between three and five minutes long, and I recommend that you create a video view audience of anyone who has watched at least 25% of any of those videos. This means people will drop into your audience if they watch around a minute of your video. If you've held someone's attention for that long on social media, they're highly engaged and relevant.

Video is the ultimate medium for content distribution, because you can demonstrate your values quickly and people can get to know you before they even meet you. If it is done correctly, video can build that rapport and relationship quickly. This is especially true of live video, a recent addition that generates more engagement and connection than pre-recorded video. It's easy to create a video, and you can repurpose it for other mediums and across multiple platforms. If you feel uncomfortable in front of the camera, the secret is merely practice. You're not looking to win an Oscar or to record perfect videos. If anything, presenting the raw and authentic version of yourself is a much more effective way of conveying your values and building that bond.

Native video content is also one of the cheapest ways to build a relevant audience. To capture a traditional lead though an opt-in process will cost you between around £2.50 and £5, depending on your niche. If it costs you £5 a lead for the opt-in, you've then got to deliver your lead magnet and get someone to consume it. In my experience, only around 50% of people who ask for your lead magnet will actually open the email that delivers it. If we assume that everyone who opens that email downloads the lead magnet, it actually costs you £10 a download before a consumer even reads and actions the lead magnet. When I run video view campaigns, I often find that each view of 25% of a five-minute video costs less than 20p, and each view of the whole video costs less than 30p.

Who do you think is more relevant and engaged with you and your message: the person who's clicked on an ad and requested a report, or the person who's watched a five-minute video on Facebook and resisted the myriad of other distractions that they have been offered? That video view is highly valuable, and it costs only a fraction of the cost of getting an opt-in.

Magnetisers

Now you've attracted and captured the most relevant audiences for you, the next step is to magnetise them to your message and develop deep rapport, quickly. Essentially, to fall into your engagement audiences, someone has (metaphorically) put their hand up and told you they have a problem that you can fix, and they're interested in what you can do for them.

So far, all you've had is fleeting contact. They're interested, but they're not sold. If the person doesn't hear from you again soon, your message will quickly fade into the background. But because you've now created your engagement-based audiences, you can communicate with them on your terms, and you can set up systems to ensure that you show up, consistently, with a message tailored to them.

Robert Cialdini describes the psychological principle 'pre-suasion', which is when your brain makes a link between what it's focusing on and causality.[2] Put simply, if you show up regularly and you draw the mind's attention, the viewer will associate you with having the ability to make things happen. Woody Allen famously said that 80% of success is down to just showing up,[3] and that principle applies here. By showing up consistently you will rapidly raise your credibility and authority, because your audience is forced to take note of your message and it sticks in their mind.

---

2   R. Cialdini, *Pre-Suasion: A Revolutionary Way to Influence and Persuade* (Random House Business, 2017)

3   T.J. Peters and R.H. Waterman Jr., *In Search of Excellence: Lessons from America's Best-Run Companies* (HarperBusiness Essentials: HarperCollins, 2004, reprint of 1982 edn)

How do you create a consistent presence without spending your entire life posting snaps on Facebook and Instagram? The answer lies in building a hybrid of systems and community. In other words, you need to automate the distribution of your core content and create a community will distribute it further for you.

Nurture method 1: The autoresponder

If you're collecting email addresses, the natural place to start with your follow-up is an automated email sequence. Most people either have no follow-up at all or they have one that defaults to a direct sales call to action from day one, extracting goodwill from the bank they've built up.

If you're selling high-ticket services, it's important to build a relationship in the right way. Your automated email sequences should start by leading the reader through the pain, problem and process narrative again, while introducing you and your values. Although I outsource all the copy that goes onto my webpages, I write all my own emails to make sure my voice and values come through. Create engagement in your emails by asking questions to prompt a response. People on your email list are not just stats to be converted; they are real people and you must build a connection with them. This may sound like hard work, but when you're getting started that personal touch will elevate you above your competitors. Automation is not a way to abdicate every function in your business while you spend the rest of your life on the beach – this couldn't be further from the truth. The real point of automation is to connect you to the right person, at the right place, at the right time. At that point, the human connection is needed to turn the lead into a lifetime client. The automation serves as a filter.

Autoresponders are not limited to emails. If you're using a chatbot, for example, you can mirror your messaging and sequences from your email autoresponder. You will need to repurpose them so that they are in a much shorter form and in a tone of voice that's appropriate for social media.

When you are automating your nurture sequences, make sure you include regular links to other elements of your content to create that open loop of value. By 'bouncing' your readers across multiple platforms to different contact points, you are increasing the perception that you are everywhere and reinforcing the concept of 'what's focal is causal'.

Nurture method 2: Text messaging

There are numerous text message services that would require your lead to provide their phone number when requesting your lead magnet. At the time of writing, text message marketing is still largely unadopted as a medium, which makes it extremely effective at commanding attention. When a text message comes in, we almost always look at it.

It does cost money to send text messages, so it is a medium to be used sparingly. In addition, you don't want to erode goodwill by inundating your lead with marketing texts. Use it for a direct call to action from within your ecosystem; for example, if you're putting on a deep dive training session, if you're running a discovery day or even for sales messages – with a 'money off' sale, for example.

If you're hosting a discovery day event, especially if it's a free one, always ask for the mobile number as part of the sign-up process. You can then integrate additional touch points in the run-up to the event in order to increase attendance rates. Some text messaging services allow two-way messaging so that you or your team can ask for real-time feedback or answer questions using the text platform. You will also have the mobile number for future promotions; for example, you could use it to notify your 'hot list' when you're launching new events, programmes or services.

Nurture method 3: Direct mail

Another overlooked part of your ecosystem is direct mail. This is where you send something physical to your audience, whether it's a book, a report, an invitation or even a box full of cool stuff. This creates a 'thud factor' when it arrives, and it will also have a longer shelf life. Many people delete emails and PDFs, but a piece of mail will often sit on a desk or a shelf for a considerable length of time, occupying mind space at a subconscious level. You can do a lot to customise direct mail for the recipient; for example, you could include a short, handwritten note, which will instantly increase your bond. There is a real opportunity to stand out by sending your audience items that reflect your (and their) values.

To integrate direct mail into your ecosystem, you need to get the postal address in the first place. This is usually too much to ask in exchange for an initial lead magnet. There's a simple way of doing this, which is just to ask for the address. In my experience, the take up of direct mail is high: few other service providers offer it, so if you have something of value to offer, people will request it. Once you have a physical mailing address, you can follow up with more refined calls to action.

The disadvantage of using direct mail is the higher cost associated with it – just look at the price of stamps these days! Like text messages, you should reserve direct mail for your hottest leads. Create a subsection of your audience, based on their engagement, to offer a piece of direct mail. It's easy to segment this across platforms using the same techniques outlined in the sections on attractors. For example, you could share a new content video with your existing audiences, then send a call to action to the subsection that watches it, giving them the opportunity to request your physical resource.

Nurture method 4: The Facebook group

In early 2018, Mark Zuckerberg announced he was looking to bring Facebook back to its roots so that users could experience more 'meaningful social interactions' instead of seeing media posts from business pages.[4] Facebook then rolled out a new algorithm designed to reduce the organic reach of content from business pages and increase the reach of content that was getting a high level of engagement. To achieve this, it focused on the Facebook group – a community of people who are engaging and interacting with each other. Although it can be labour-intensive, creating and nurturing a Facebook group can build you a relevant community of people, with higher levels of engagement, who not only view you as the authority (as the group leader) but also see more of the content posted in the group (because the algorithm rewards it).

There are two types of Facebook group: an open group, which anyone can join; or a closed group, where you control who has access. Which group you choose will depend on your niche and your goals within the group, but I prefer to have a closed group that requires new

---

4   M. Zuckerberg, Facebook (2018) www.facebook.com/zuck/posts
/10104413015393571?pnref=story

members to answer three questions when they join. The questions act as a filter to ensure that only the most relevant people are joining, building a smaller but stronger community.

If you create your own group, you must not view it as a sales opportunity and spend your time pitching to the group members. It must be a community that you are curating and growing, where members get a lot of value and a sense of belonging. When you do this right, the authority you gain by running the group will lead people to reach out to you as they ascend themselves through your system. If you don't create engagement in your group, the algorithm will punish you by restricting the reach of the content you share within it.

Nurture method 5: Total domination

Total domination isn't as sinister as it might sound. It's about making sure you get your content in front of your social media audience in a consistent, automated and scalable way. This strategy has been a game changer for many of my clients. Here's how it works.

The 'Attractors' section explained how to build audiences based on engagement, who you can follow up with. You can enhance this by making these audiences 'time-bound', creating multiple groups based on the length of time since their initial engagement. The next step is to set up different campaigns where you pay to distribute your core content to these varying time-bound audiences. You can select what content is sent to each audience depending on how long ago they interacted.

Put simply, you can build a narrative by deciding what content people are going to see after they have engaged with you for the first time. Set this campaign up so that immediately after someone engages with you, they will see content that raises awareness of the pain/problem gap. After a certain amount of time, you can start to show them content that is focused on your solution to their problem and demonstrates your values so that your time-bound audience gets to know the real you. You then start to introduce pure authority-building content: testimonials from others and social proof. Finally, you can introduce some calls to action to ascend your audience to the next stage of your process.

The beauty of this strategy is that every time you develop another piece of core content under your three pillars of messaging, you can add it to your total domination campaign. When you've written it once, Facebook will show it to the right people over and over again, removing the need to be constantly creating and posting new content. You can even control how often people will see your content, so if you want your audience to see two posts from you every day, you can tell Facebook to do that.

This whole process is so simple. After you've defined and built the audiences you want to distribute your content to, all you need to do is post on your page and add it to your campaign, taking about sixty seconds.

Imagine that! Someone finds your video on Facebook, watches the whole video because the message resonates with them, drops into your engagement audience and then sees content from you every day for the next three months. They're learning from you and you are developing trust and rapport with them by being consistent. It doesn't take long until they feel as if they know you, and then it's only a matter of time before they reach out to connect with you in person.

Primers and the call to action

At some point, you will need to put a call to action in front of your audience to ascend them into your product ecosystem. It's important to get this right; you don't want to destroy all the goodwill and rapport that you've worked so hard to build. All too often I've seen experts develop high levels of trust through their content, but when it comes to making offers, they find it difficult to switch from delivering value to making a sale.

To avoid this trap, you must switch from marketing to sales in a way that maintains integrity, doesn't deposition you and is a seamless experience for your audience. The best way to do this is to 'prime' your lead to accept the principle of the offer you're about to make. To do this, you use a piece of 'primer content'. Typical primer content could include:

- A webinar

- On-demand video training

- An in-person event

Privileged moments

The mind can only focus on one thing at a time. (We can multi-task, but the brain is rapidly switching between tasks rather than performing multiple tasks concurrently.) It follows that when we have the focused attention of a mind, it is shut off to non-related concepts vying for attention. At the same time, it is also open to related, or secondary concepts.

Because the mind works in this way, before you make a call to action you need to grab the focused attention of the brain and close it off to the myriad of other distractions and messages competing for its attention. Primer content is designed to do exactly that, capturing and holding the mind's attention while creating what Cialdini calls a 'privileged moment'.[5]

---

5 R. Cialdini, *Pre-Suasion: A Revolutionary Way to Influence and Persuade* (Random House Business, 2017)

A privileged moment is a finite amount of time when the brain is focusing on the concepts you've presented to it. While the brain is absorbing these concepts, it is willing to accept secondary concepts, such as a call to action. If you fail to present a call to action in this 'privileged moment', the mind will resume its distracted state and is less likely to follow the course of action you are hoping for.

This is why at physical sales events, scarcity is so often used to bring an audience to the point of signing up to a programme or service. When someone is at a conference for a few days, their brain is entirely focused on the concepts that are being presented, and a privileged moment has been created. The problem is that often, the audience's action is stimulated by a fear of missing out on a 'deal', rather than the transformational outcome you provide. This scarcity is often false, and, because the audience has only been with you for a short period of time, they have not gone through the awareness and authority cycle. This has a knock-on effect on results.

By providing primer content, we can replicate this privileged moment after someone has been in your ecosystem and has all of the pieces of the puzzle in front of them. As you build your value ecosystem, you should integrate primer content into it on a regular basis so members of your audience can ascend when they are ready.

Structuring primer content

It's important to focus on a framework for your primer content before you consider the script. Here is the framework I use for all my primer content, whether it's a thirty-minute video or a two-day discovery event:

- **Introduction.** Set the scene by introducing yourself, why you're qualified to be delivering the content and what the audience is going to learn.

- **Pain.** Emphasise the pain that the audience is experiencing.

- **Problem.** Bridge the gap between the pain and the underlying problem that the audience has. This brings them to the point of illumination.

- **Consequence.** Highlight the consequences of not solving this problem.

- **Story.** Emphasise the point by introducing your story and how you've arrived at this point in your life and business. It is much easier for your audience to relate to concepts, and to believe them, when they are told as a story, because stories are more engaging than facts and figures.

- **Process.** Centre the bulk of the training around your unique process, which we developed in Chapter 4.

- **Outcome.** Ensure that your audience can visualise how your solution will improve their lives.

- **Social proof.** Use case studies about other people to add credibility to your message.

- **Call to action.** Explain the next step the audience needs to take to ascend into your product ecosystem.

When you make your call to action, keep it authentic and congruent with everything you've done so far. If you've built your value ecosystem correctly and nurtured your audience through your open loop of content, you won't need to use scarcity or manipulation to encourage them to take action. Instead, you want people to ascend through your 'calls to action' because they have a burning desire to work with you and achieve the outcome you're offering. By following the Triple A Method and building out your value ecosystem, you will make this happen. Not only that, but you will be working with the best clients who are committed to getting results.

Summary

In this final chapter we have looked at the real-world tactics that are available to build your value ecosystem right now. The chapter is not exhaustive and the methods available to us change on a regular basis. I suggest that you take the value ecosystem framework and find out what tactics work for you within it.

Regardless of the tactics you use, the foundational principle here is the need to attract a relevant audience, have the ability to capture that audience and then magnetise it with open loop value before ascending those people to become paying clients.

When you use this framework, you will accelerate your own authority and become an irresistible solution provider to your market.

CHAPTER EIGHT: EXERCISES

To create your attractor piece of content, whether it's a report, video training or webinar, answer these questions, which will guide the structure:

1. What is the problem you solve? Describe, in detail, three painful areas (or pain points) of this problem. These are actions they might take that remind them of their problem.

2. What will happen if they don't solve this problem? How do you solve this problem?

3. How is your solution different from what your lead may have experienced before?

4. When someone solves their problem using their solution, what are the results they will see? What is the next step they can take after reading this guide/watching this training?

Conclusion

You should now have a thorough understanding of how to use the Triple A Method by building your own value ecosystem. This book has explained that the expert industry is rapidly changing: in a world where it is more difficult to command attention, with markets that are more sophisticated, we need to adapt our methods to show our authentic selves and the transformational outcomes we provide.

Regardless of our expert abilities, however, none of it matters unless we can reach the right people, at the right time, in the right state. The Triple A Method will achieve this for you by creating awareness in your market of the real problems and your unique methods of solving them; boosting your authority through demonstration, association and education; and automating the audience-building, attraction and ascension processes so you can scale your impact and profits.

This book has explored some real-world tools and methods that you can use to achieve these results yourself. None of these tools are expensive or require technical expertise; anyone can use them set up their own value ecosystem.

What's next?

You can transform your business and your life by becoming the most sought-after authority in your niche. By continually raising your own level of authority, you will attract better clients in greater numbers, be able to raise your prices, attract more opportunities and have more fun than ever before.

Authority is not something that is bestowed on you. You can reach out and create it yourself by following the frameworks explained in this book. Building authority is simple, but it is rarely easy. You will need to work hard to achieve it, and the process will push you out of your comfort zone. On difficult days you'll question why you're doing it.

Don't be put off by this, because the flip side is a transformation of your life. Not just for you, but for your family, your marketplace and, perhaps, wider society. As expert entrepreneurs, we all have a duty to expand our reach and influence to help more people than just ourselves. Our world is rapidly evolving, and people need guidance and support. You have the opportunity to provide that support: you get to make a difference *and* make more profit in the process.

Here are some techniques for success to keep you on track:

1. Make time to create content

You can rapidly increase your content production and visibility by spending just one hour a week on creating content. When you really focus, you can create one or two pieces of high-quality content in that time.

The trick is to view creating content as a 'must do' activity, rather than a 'nice to do' activity. This will stop you putting it off and help you focus your attention. I set protected time in my diary every week to create content. I enter it into my iCal and set up reminders to make me accountable. In this protected time, I am not allowed to open my email, browse social media or be distracted by texts or phone calls. As with all change, it is hard to begin with, but it's a high-performance habit you need to get into.

I find it helpful to create my content first thing in the morning, before the world gets to work and starts to insert the long screwdriver of distraction into my day. If you can manage to do a thirty-minute session twice a week, six months from now you'll have a huge content library.

2. Be consistent

An overnight success takes many years to create. But you can accelerate the process by using the techniques outlined in this book.

The key to your success is consistency. Consistency of presence, of message and of building your audiences. If you have an offer that your market wants and you communicate it well, you can be a huge success. But you have to put in the time to build audiences of people who know, like and trust you and who are ready to buy.

Your authority growth curve is likely to be parabolic. In other words, it will look flat for longer than you want it to while you're putting your systems in place and gaining momentum, but then it will rise steeply. This is the nature of authority growth: don't give up just before the pay-off happens. If you follow the system, it *will* work for you.

3. Be congruent with your message

To build true authority, you need to be true to yourself and your unique set of values. If you feel that you're not worthy or that you're going to be 'found out', this will come across in what you project, and your audience will pick up on it. When you have an unwavering belief in what you're doing, you will exude confidence and become an irresistibly attractive force.

To be congruent with what you're doing, you need to understand your purpose, have a vision for what you're creating and have a mission that you're working towards. Gaining this understanding of yourself is not easy and takes time, so it's important to start reflecting now.

4. Live life on your terms

This is the most important advice I can give you. This process of building your expert business and raising your authority should challenge you, but it should also be fun. We have but one life, so I urge you to grasp it with both hands and run with it. My only fear is to leave this world with regrets and without trying to take opportunities, even if they don't pan out.

One of the strongest intrinsic drivers for humans is the need for autonomy: to control how we live our lives. The only way to create true autonomy is to build a business around the lifestyle we want to lead, whether your goal is to create an international training company or to be able to have breakfast with your kids every day of the week.

When you live life on your terms, you'll start to find that you work in flow and everything becomes effortless.

I wish you every success in your journey to becoming the go-to authority in your marketplace. While the tactics of how to achieve this will change over time, the frameworks will not. Focus on using the Triple A Method in everything you do, and see your results explode.

References

Albrecht, K., 'The (Only) 5 Fears We All Share' (*Psychology Today*, 2012), www.psychologytoday.com/gb/blog/brainsnacks/201203/the-only-5-fears-we-all-share

Cialdini, R., *Pre-Suasion: A Revolutionary Way to Influence and Persuade* (Random House Business, 2017)

Peters, T.J. and Waterman Jr., R.H., *In Search of Excellence: Lessons from America's Best-Run Companies* (HarperBusiness Essentials: HarperCollins, 2004, reprint of 1982 edn)

Zuckerberg, M., Facebook post, 12 January (2018), www.facebook.com/zuck/posts/10104413015393571?pnref=story

The Author

 Robert Stewart served as a fast jet pilot in the RAF for twelve years, first as an air defence pilot on the Tornado F3 and then as a tactics and weapons instructor on the Hawk. His final tour was on exchange with the South African Air Force, helping to train their pilots.

It was here that Rob first discovered his passion for training and mentoring others, a purpose that would go on to shape his business career.

After leaving the RAF in 2012, Rob started to grow a buy-to-let property portfolio in the north-west of the UK. He soon discovered that he wanted to continue his career in training and founded the Property Education Group (PEG), which helped property entrepreneurs set up systemised and leverageable businesses.

PEG grew quickly, mainly thanks to the methods that Rob used to position it within the property space. At the same time, Rob saw that fellow speakers and trainers were struggling to reach their own markets. He then founded V Media Global, a training and marketing company with a mission to help 10,000 expert entrepreneurs reach and positively influence 10,000 people each, and so move a nation.

🌐 www.robstewartglobal.com

The Authority Class

Now you've read this book, the ideal next step is to take a deeper dive into how to build your authority, craft a premium priced offer and build your own value ecosystem by registering for the Authority Class.

This on-demand training will help you reach a greater level of self-awareness and understanding in your own business so you can identify the areas you need to focus on before showing you how to rapidly raise your intrinsic value.

www.authorityclass.com